Black Women Mothering & Daughtering During a Dual Pandemic

Writing Our Backs

A Volume in Research, Advocacy, Collaboration, and
Empowerment Mentoring Series

Series Editor

Donna Y. Ford
Ohio State University

Black Women Mothering & Daughtering During a Dual Pandemic

Writing Our Backs

Editors

Venus E. Evans-Winters
*Ohio State University &
African American Policy Forum*

Amber Jean-Marie Pabon
Kutztown University

Theresa Y. Robinson
Elmhurst University

≡IAP

INFORMATION AGE PUBLISHING, INC.
Charlotte, NC • www.infoagepub.com

Library of Congress Cataloging-in-Publication Data

CIP record for this book is available from the Library of Congress
http://www.loc.gov

ISBNs: 979-8-88730-468-7 (Paperback)

         979-8-88730-469-4 (Hardcover)

         979-8-88730-470-0 (ebook)

Printed in the United States of America

CONTENTS

FOREWORD

Michelle Frazier Trotman Scott

In 2013, I, along with Dr. Donna Y. Ford and Dr. Malik Henfield, co-founded Research, Advocacy, Collaboration, Empowerment (R.A.C.E) Mentoring, a private social media mentoring group that catalyzed support and advocacy for doctoral students, junior and untenured faculty, and tenured faculty of color. In this nurturing space, I met Dr. Venus Evans-Winters, affectionately known as Dr. V, and we embarked upon a relationship that transcended the boundaries of academia. Dr. V's research and area of focus are that of social and cultural foundations of education, Black feminist thought, critical race theory, educational policy, and qualitative inquiry, along with her experience as a psychotherapist, a certified clinical trauma professional, and school social worker, and youth advocate, she is the ideal first author of this work—the collaborative co-editing efforts of Drs. Evans-Winters, Pabon, and Robinson brought forth a book that will provide its readers with insight and a sense of camaraderie between themselves and other Black women as they navigate life.

The dual pandemics of COVID-19 and racial injustice will represent some of the most defining moments in history. In this book's pages, I witness an extraordinary journey that highlights the spirit of Black women and the transformative potential of literature, conversation, and solidarity. Through the lens of a Black women's mental health literature circle, the authors of the chapters share stories, collective reflection, and mutual support. This circle became a lifeline and a source of strength for women during a global health crisis and the persistent shadows of racial inequity. It became a space of solace, connection, and healing.

Amidst the turbulence and isolation of a world thrust into uncertainty by the global COVID-19 pandemic, Dr. Evans-Winters created a virtual refuge, a space for Black women to gather, connect, and find sustenance for their minds and spirits. The virtual weekly meetings of this literature circle served as a profound reminder that despite the physical distance that separated them, the shared experiences of being Black women navigating their complexities united them in purpose and solidarity.

The literature circle endeavored to explore the literature authored by Black women and to serve as a conduit for dialogue, introspection, and collective growth. Books such as Alice Walker's *The Temple of My Familiar* and Tressie McMillan Cottom's *Thick* served as both stories to be read and as mirrors to reflect the participants' lived experiences. Each chapter serves as a narrative of a woman who embarked on a journey of self-discovery, confronting themes of identity, resilience, and her existence as a mother, daughter, sister, girlfriend, and wife.

The stories unfolding within these pages are a testament to the power of unity, resilience, and collective action. It is a testament to the enduring strength of Black women, who emerged as pillars of support for one another and beacons of hope for their communities in the face of unprecedented challenges. Their journey inspires us all, reminding us that even amidst the darkest times, the human spirit can rise, connect, and transform.

Literature has the power to surpass the boundaries of time and space. When reading people can immerse themselves in the thoughts and emotions of characters who mirror their aspirations and struggles. The literature circle found liberation, empathy, and a sense of unity within the pages of selected books. As they delved into the books crafted by Black women authors, their joys and sorrows, triumphs and setbacks, challenges, and victories were echoed on each page.

The literature circle was more than an exploration of literature; it evolved into a sanctuary that allowed the nurturing of the mind, body, and spirit. The sessions offered a respite from the outside world's discord and an opportunity for self-reflection. Each woman could self-express, channel their emotions and experiences, and transform their pain into beauty and resilience.

The heart of this literature circle, though, lay in the deep, meaningful dialogues that transcended the boundaries of the virtual realm. With Dr. Evans-Winters's guidance and leadership, the authors created a safe space where testimonies of personal experiences were shared openly and honestly. These conversations allowed the women to affirm their shared levels of compassion and forged connections rooted in understanding and sisterhood.

The narratives of the literature circle participants unfold within the pages of the book, with their voices, perspectives, and reflections resonating with the complexities of Black womanhood. Their stories are a testament to the resilience and strength of Black women who, despite the weight of dual pandemics, emerged as pillars of support for one another. Their testimonies reflect various experiences amidst the challenges of COVID-19 and demonstrate their collective determination to dismantle the oppressive structures of racial injustice.

As we delve into the stories chronicled within these pages, we must recognize the transformative power of these Black women's experiences and acknowledge their universal truth. Their resilience serves as a guiding light and reminds us that even in the darkest times, there is strength in the connection of and healing in shared stories, and hope is found in the pursuit of justice.

ACKNOWLEDGEMENTS

This project could not have been accomplished without the support of Planet Venus and The Black Women's Mental Wealth Group (BWMH). We thank Dr. Venus Evans Winters for her wisdom, leadership, and tireless efforts to elevate our thinking. We are also grateful to Dr. Donna Ford for supporting the publication of this book. Dr. Evans-Winters' and Ford's research and training were integral to the development of this project. Lastly, the completion of this project could not have been accomplished without the contributions of the authors in specialized chapter writing and participation in a collaborative internal peer review process. We give thanks to all our family members who encouraged us as we wrote this book. We especially honor all of our ancestors who did not live to see the publication of this book, including Ms. Deloris Tomlin, Mr. Ollie Watson Jr., and Mrs. Kay Brown.

Black Women Mothering & Daughtering During a Dual Pandemic:
Writing Our Backs, pp. xiii–xiii
Copyright © 2024 by Information Age Publishing
www.infoagepub.com

INTRODUCTION

The contributors of this volume share with the scholarly community the ways in which we have learned to strive, resist, adapt, and re-conceptualize Black women's mental health and labor during the dual pandemics of white supremacy and COVID-19. The book is unique in that it calls for the contributing authors to draw upon and reflect on the use of sisterhood and a literature circle to cope with an economic crisis, mass death, and racial battle fatigue during a worldwide pandemic. Specifically, the invited authors draw inspiration from Venus E. Evans-Winters' book *Black Feminism in Qualitative Inquiry: A Mosaic for Writing Our Daughter's Body* as an exemplar of research that both centers the issues and concerns of Black women scholar-practitioner-activists and presents a methodology consistent with Black feminist ways of knowing and expressions. Evans-Winters's theoretical and methodological writings are among the first works in research and gender studies that successfully interweaved Black feminists' politics, spirituality, and Africanism with educational research and thought. The text dynamically weaves themes uniquely relevant to Black women's lives, including our socialization and socio-emotional development, mother/ othermother-daughter relationships, navigating the racial politics of schooling, friendships, socio-emotional development, survivorship, and grief into constructed stories that demonstrate non-normative methodological concepts and practices.

The authors explore concepts such as *daughtering, politicking, motherspeak,* and *cultural exchange,* which comprise some of the concepts explored by authors while also including linguistic expressions such as prose, text messages, dialogue, and personal narrative—all firmly planted in authentic Black womanist aesthetics. Furthermore, authors were called to highlight

Black Women Mothering & Daughtering During a Dual Pandemic:
Writing Our Backs, pp. xv–xvi
Copyright © 2024 by Information Age Publishing
www.infoagepub.com

and demonstrate *why* and *how* they use reading and Black women's literary works to critically reflect, meaningfully write, heal, and/or do Black women's work in times of *peril* (Morrison, 2019). The authors use the terms sister circle and literature circle interchangeably to refer to our collective experience.

More specifically, the book explores and discusses how other women are reading/writing and interweaving the tradition of Black women's (cultural) literacies into teaching, healing, mentoring, activism, justice work, and so forth. Throughout the book, the question raised is: How are Black women's literary works as a body of knowledge being used in healing spaces to marshal new or forgotten healing methodologies, cultural frames of references, and spiritual awakenings? The contributing authors address this question from multiple perspectives, such as education, social work, and psychology.

CHAPTER 1

DAUGHTERS SURVIVING PANDEMICS WHILE TEACHING AND HEALING

A Conversation on the Black Hand Side

Venus E. Evans-Winters and Janice Baines

Even in intense moments such as a global health and anti-Black racial pandemic, Black women have been required to shapeshift as we balance our roles as nurturers, connectors, and care providers. This chapter, as evidenced throughout the book, discusses how communal circles serve to protect our spiritual, cultural, intellectual, and mental health. Specifically, this chapter explores the following questions:

1. What is a collective Black women's community, and what role, if any, does it play in mitigating white supremacy and patriarchy?
2. How might Black women's literary works and intellectual thought help facilitate a habit of writing to heal personally and professionally? We offer ideas, thoughts, and reflections in an authentic conversation as we navigate various spaces while teaching and healing. Grounded in works by Black authors and using a Black feminist lens, readers will learn communal healing through a sister circle.

Black Women Mothering & Daughtering During a Dual Pandemic:
Writing Our Backs, pp. 1–9
Copyright © 2024 by Information Age Publishing
www.infoagepub.com

Introduction

Even in intense moments, such as a global health and anti-Black racial pandemic, Black women have been required to shapeshift as they balance their roles as nurturers, community builders, and care providers. This chapter discusses how we created communal circles across and within spaces to serve, protect, and repair relationships and take care of our own spiritual, cultural, intellectual, and mental health. Grounded in Black women's intellectual thought (Collins, 2022; Phillips, 2006; Smith, 1985) and caregiving practices, we offer ideas, thoughts, and reflections in an authentic dialogue as we navigate various spaces while teaching and healing.

Sister circles simultaneously redefine and re-imagine traditional modes of healing. U.S. culture tends to focus on healing on the individual and primarily views healing as a unidirectional process. In contrast, sister circles are created to be communal spaces embedded in (a) resistance practices and (b) processes of resilience (Dunmeyer et al., 2022). Drawing upon the Black feminist practice of sister circles, we use the phrase *communal circles* interchangeably to capture how we center: (1) resistance and resilience, (2) gender and cultural ways of knowing, and (3) rites and rituals. In other words, we extend the conversation of the possibility of sister circles beyond a focus on literacy engagement with the text(s) and more toward a playing with the embodiment of histories crafted upon our bodies and psyches.

As such, we reflect upon the role that our overlapping identities as Black women and daughters (and sisters/mothers/aunties) play in reclaiming the center in our home places and "choosing the margins" (hooks, 2015) in our workspaces. In the discussion, we use call-and-response, which is grounded in the African American oral tradition, to share ideas, thoughts, and reflections. We hope that readers can capture the organic gender and culturally embodied coping strategies we relied upon as the multiply vulnerable to survive teaching/learning and suffering/healing during a global pandemic. We employed critical reflexivity (see Kessler, 2020) to better understand how our relationships as daughters helped us thrive during a historical moment of human suffering and refuge from racial capitalism.

Critical reflexivity is grounded in the ethos of critical race pedagogy (Lynn et al., 2013), critical race feminism in education (Evans-Winters & Esposito, 2010), and intersectional qualitative inquiry as well as teacher education and social work practice. Critical dialogue allows the opportunity to openly and authentically reflect alongside another sister/daughter to better understand how our individual lived experiences unveil a shared cultural experience. Shared cultural experiences serve the purpose of documenting our humanity and collective resilience in the face of gender and racial oppression.

Venus (Daughter/Mother): How might sister circles interrupt traditional notions of healing, especially since we tend to think of healing as a one-direction process that takes place with one healer and one person in need of healing?

Venus

Lock-down. That was the word that stood out to me. It reminded me of jail, no, prisons. Governments put people in prisons to control our bodies and reprogram our minds. This time, it was not the government but this strange virus that was locking me down in my own home. I like my home; it is comfortable, warm, and familiar. What was not comfortable was that the "lockdown" required me to be more aware of my body. Not only my physical body but my mind, too. Hell, I can cope with quarantine because I was not much of a person who had to dine out at restaurants, be present at the next girlfriends' gathering, or even be seen in a club with a lot of people.

For me, I was forced to pay attention to everything that I hated about seclusion, which was keeping my mind unoccupied and making my body sit. The virus forced me to pay attention to my body: Am I physically active enough? Will I gain weight? Will we run out of food? What about basic necessities like water, toilet paper, canned goods.........................? How often and for how long should I be washing my hands? Are these white people going to lose their minds and start breaking into our homes or hoarding scarce goods? Through mindfulness and meditation, I trained myself to be more conscientious of my body while not being tied to my body. Still, here it was: this virus was forcing me once again to worry about something beyond my control, and it had me thinking about it every minute of the day with no distractions.

How did I cope in the past with feelings of lack of control? "I can drink to pass the time!"

After a while, I knew that was not an option because I decided to stop abusing alcohol a long time ago, and I could not drink and continue to do my work as a therapist and professor during this public health crisis.

Plan B. I've always turned to reading, writing, and intellectual stimulation to escape this world while also using what I had learned to help heal others. "Got it!" I can combine my love of reading with the act of helping heal other women. "A reading circle!"

Janice (Daughter/Sister)

As the severity of the pandemic became evident, schools closed, but teaching students still had to go on. As teachers, the worry was constant about how we would serve students during the immediate transition to online instruction, even though students, families, and educators did not have the equipment or capacity to meet the new expectations. Before the pandemic, many perceived teachers as "non-essential" and "disposable"—taken for granted even. Yet, our status quickly changed, and the recognition that teachers are *essential* became evident.

In the midst of e-learning, virtual platforms, and parent/student accountability, the blame game began, and, as a teacher, I realized that I was just a pawn—a person who could be criticized for students not doing well. My 12-hour days became 16 overnight as I tried to reconfigure my instruction from in-person to online. Still, no plan fit what each child or family needed—no one thought to provide the students with electronic devices. Pressing questions from the media and school were constant. Who would care for the children if parents had to work? How would this pandemic affect everyone's finances if people could not work and be paid? Every day, there was something different, but INSTRUCTION had to continue. I never questioned it. I was on autopilot. Zoom, FaceTime, and Facebook Messenger were the new trends.

Somehow, I trudged forth and conquered what was needed to assist all of my students. But I failed in my own home. I was seeking space from this *new normal* COVID-19 created. Teaching, graduate school, and life harbored most of my mind. There was no sacred space, and my mind, body, and spirit were bombarded with worries and stress.

Then, I received an unexpected email from Dr. Venus Evans-Winters, affectionately referred to as Dr. V., inviting me to a reading circle.

Amid the panic that accompanied the pandemics, I had forgotten how much I loved reading and how much it soothed me. A reading circle composed of Black women (sister circle) would give me a reprieve from the daily arduous tasks piled so high I could not see beyond them. I needed to be able to read something that reminded me of who I am. So, to heal myself so I could effectively teach my students and care for my family, I enthusiastically responded, "Hi, Dr. V. Thank you for the invitation, and this is necessary. I will order my books tonight and will see you all Friday." This sister circle saved my life and sanity. It provided refuge and support. The sister circle provided mental wealth support amid the changing landscape of teaching that I was thrust into. During this pivotal moment in history, my intersecting identities as a Black woman, daughter, auntie, and teacher required centering as essential for sustainability at work and home. How could the sister circle have a meaningful impact amid the craziness?

The process of reading, discussing questions, delivering lessons, and writing was incredibly enriching. These activities contributed to both my personal growth and developed my social relationships with other women. Timely, the sister circle provided a platform to connect with others, reflect on my personal experiences, and ability to work toward other much-needed personal changes. I came to realize that daughtering, other mothering, and sister circles are physical manifestations of our spiritual work.

In this manner, sister circles are kindred sanctuary spaces (Smith, 2016). The sister circle also created an appreciation of the power and potential for collective healing. The wisdom from authors such as Toni Morrison, Alice Walker, Tressie Cottom, and our sister-circle convener and visionary of this co-edited book, Dr. Venus E. Evans-Winters, impacted my understanding of the power of Black women's literary spaces. They reminded me that such spaces are invaluable and can build community, create a sense of belonging, and foster healing.

Venus (Daughter/Mother): What role do Black women's intersectional and overlapping identities play in reclaiming the center in our home spaces and claiming the margins in workspaces that privilege whiteness and authoritarianism?

Janice: Black women have to be all things to so many people and are expected to do everything. So, by default, and perhaps by design, we hold and maintain the center. Being a Black Baptist educator and woman, I have had multiple roles ingrained in me since my existence. Black is the robe that I wear, polished with the strength of my ancestors. It is bold, loud, and full of wisdom. Baptist, the carrier and connector to my God, the highest. Woman, the origin and giver of life; nurturer and lover. With age, the identities overlapped and strengthened for me to navigate in my home fluently. I knew my role. Being black and a woman became equivalent to being a superhero. I needed the undercover identity to escape the unnecessary, though essential, pressures of caring for and teaching 20–25 children each year.

JANICE: A DAUGHTERING ARTIFACT

As I reflect on my multiple roles as a Black, Christian, relatively young (36) woman, I search for the origin and source of the expectation (real or imagined) that Black women have to do it all. Do we, as Black women, impose this on ourselves, or do other people think this, so we feel we have to prove it? What messages have we internalized? I don't know where that stems from, but it's a heavy, dark cloud that is omnipresent. Real. I don't know a single Black girl/woman who has not internalized the message that Black women have to be smarter, faster, stronger, and so forth. We are sent messages from our families, churches, and social media, which convey the sentiment *it's your turn. Get it done.*

I would be remiss if I did not comment on the complicated, warring weight and joy of being Black in an anti-Black society, where scrutiny, disrespect, and ridicule are constant. Respectfully, then, I recognize that Black males also carry their burdens. However, in the final analysis, much responsibility falls at the feet of Black women—even when we do not rightly receive credit for it. For sure, I am proud to be Black and a woman, but sometimes the load is heavy. Thankfully, other Black sisters hold me up when I am weak. Women like Dr. V see my fullness, understand my reality, and know the importance of bonding with each other. That is actually our superpower.

Superpower or curse? Drawing upon The Gospel of Shug Avery, Walker (1989) wrote, "Helped are those who love the broken and the whole; none of their children, nor any of their ancestors, nor any parts of themselves shall be despised" (p. 289). Time was not on our side. It came, and we went. My cousin called, and life drastically shifted for us all in a matter of seconds.

"Hello!" I said.

"Girl, she did not come! I don't know about anyone else, but I will be pissed if something happens to MY MOMMA!" My cousin growled on the phone.

I immediately immersed myself in *daughtering* (Evans-Winters, 2019b) mode, and instantaneously, I recognized the sacrifices Grandma had made for me and my family. Slowly, my mouth fired, "You can bring Grandma here; she can stay in the room beside me." I recognized the remnants of "clean pain" (Menakem, 2017, p. 19); my cousin passed through the phone. I couldn't conceptualize Grandma experiencing any abandonment. She was my mother's mother; grandma extended herself to ensure my needs were met all my life. It was now her time to reap the benefits of her labor of love.

I nervously waited for Grandma's arrival with thoughts of our road trips and food escapes. I took one last glance at the newly arranged room before its new tenant entered. I smiled when I heard the horn of the white Ford Expedition as it pulled into the driveway. I saw a tiny straw hat leaning forward in the car's front passenger seat. "Hello, Jenice," a nickname grandma would call me for entertainment. "Hey. Grandma. I heard you're coming to let me spoil you," I responded while unfastening her seatbelt.

"I'm going to let you do that," she said with a smile. As I looked into her slender, brown eyes, I tried grappling with what this new form of "daughtering" entailed. With each movement she made to become reacquainted with the house since my mother passed away, I recognized every whimper that resulted in shared memories. I knew that she was home.

VENUS: METHODOLOGICAL ARTIFACT

Daughtering as a methodological framework is grounded in the ethos of the Black civil rights movement, Black feminism, and Black girls and women's ways of knowing and being in the world (Evans-Winters, 2019a). Living at the intersections of race, gender, and age, Black girls' socialization into Black childhood and womanhood provides them opportunities to develop habits of mind that are similar to yet uniquely different from their Black boy peers and other youth. The habits of mind help us/them navigate patriarchy and white supremacy, interracial violence in families and communities, and hostile schools and workplaces. I (Venus) have discussed in other works (see Evans-Winters, 2011; Evans-Winters, 2019b; Waters et al, 2019) how Black girls and young women's psychosocial and cultural development influences our research approaches. Below, I attempt to illustrate how daughtering influences our relationships with our women within and across communal spaces.

DAUGHTERING INTERCONNECTEDNESS

Figure 1.1

Daughtering as Interconnectedness. This Relationship Model Situates Black Women's Coping Strategies Within Traditional Girlhood Practices That Buffer Adversity During Uncertain Times

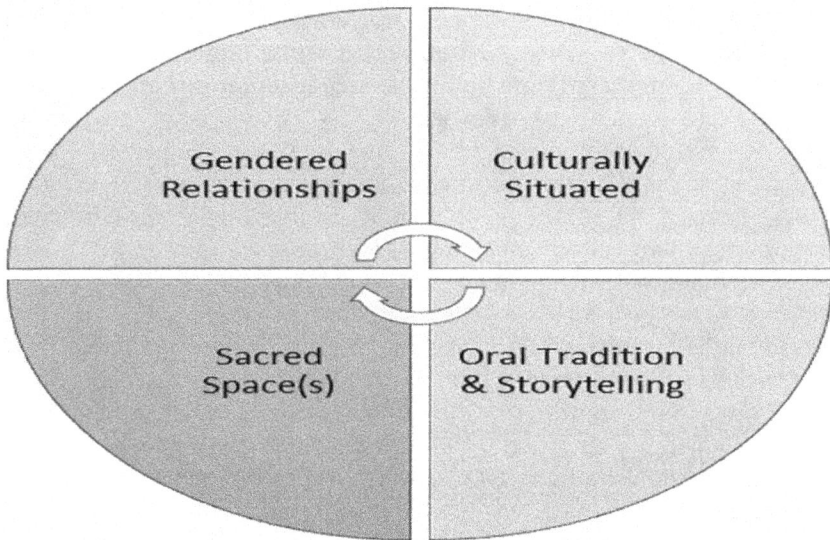

In this chapter and throughout the book, we put forth daughtering as a methodology and a praxis. During a very precarious time in human history, we figured out what we needed to positively cope while balancing our roles as daughters (or cultural beings in gendered bodies) and engaged citizens (racial and gender justice advocates and educators). Our interconnectedness/interconnectivity (Evans-Winters, 2021) as Black women, even with distance between us, was our call to home, to something familiar.

As Black women who were once Black girls, being in gendered space felt familiar to us; thus, it was only natural during a time of uncertainty that we would want to reflect and grieve in the privacy and comfort of other women. Our private spaces and stories told are situated in Black culture and the oral tradition, particularly Black women's ways of expressing pain, joy, and other complex emotions. Therefore, daughtering as an interconnected embodied communal practice looks like Black women drawing upon cultural intuition to cope during times of stress and collective trauma. Our communal space provided temporary immunity from white supremacy, which was emotionally liberating.

HOW WE WRITE OUR BACKS: IMPLICATIONS FOR BLACK WOMEN'S HEALING

She is a friend of my mind. She gathers me, man. The pieces I am, she gather them and give them back to me in all the right order. ~ Toni Morrison (2007)

In reflection, the sister circle was both transformational and inspirational for each woman actively involved and other creatives/healers in this volume. The wisdom shared from both our individual participation as a circle and the Black women authors' work, we read created a space where we could explore our multiple identities, imaginations, and personal journeys, all while *daughtering*. Collectively, daughtering reminded us through written text and voice of the power of Black women's voices and the often unspoken need for collective healing.

Furthermore, our writing circle was a reminder that Black women are not alone in our personal struggles and that writing and reading are healing modalities intuitive to Black girls and women. Our words and our ways of life as text give our life meaning. We need opportunities to contextualize our lives. Such contextualization is our weaving together of various identities, emotions, and places. Our virtual sister circles created a sense of community where we attempted to systematically make sense of the world through our own voices.

Through the act of writing, our curated space provided a brave space for us to unpack our own narratives and deepest fears. Ultimately, the sister circle is a testament to the power of Black women-centered literature, ritual work, and emotionality. In sum, how we write is how we heal; how we heal is how we perform our writing practices in community.

REFERENCES

Collins, P. H. (2022). *Black feminist thought: Knowledge, consciousness, and the politics of empowerment*. Routledge.

Dunmeyer, A. D., Shauri-Webb, K. R., & Muhammad, G. G. E. (2022). "We are not broken": Using Sista circles as resistance, liberation, and healing. *International Journal of Qualitative Studies in Education, 36*(7), 1248–1265.

Evans-Winters, V. E. (2011). *Teaching Black girls: Resiliency in urban classrooms* (2nd ed.). Peter Lang.

Evans-Winters, V. E. (2019a). *A boss chick's guide to mindfulness meditation: A workbook for Black women*. Self-Published.

Evans-Winters, V. E. (2019b). *Black feminism in qualitative inquiry: A mosaic for writing our daughter's body*. Routledge

Evans-Winters, V. E. (2021). Black women improvisations: Shifting methodological (mis) understandings within and across boundaries. *International Journal of Qualitative Studies in Education, 34*(6), 481–485.

hooks, B. (2015). Choosing the margin as a space of radical openness. In A. Garry & M. Pearsall (Eds.), *Women, knowledge, and reality* (pp. 48–55). Routledge.

Kressler, B. (2020). Critical self-reflection as disruption: A Black feminist self-study. *Journal of Culture and Values in Education, 3*(1), 21–38. https://doi.org/10.46303/jcve.03.01.2

Lynn, M., Jennings, M. E., & Hughes, S. (2013). Critical race pedagogy 2.0: Lessons from Derrick Bell. *Race Ethnicity and Education, 16*(4), 603–628.

Menakem, R. (2017). *My grandmother's hands*. Central Recovery Press.

Morrison, T. (2007). *Beloved*. Vintage Classics.

Phillips, L. (Ed.). (2006). *The womanist reader*. Taylor & Francis.

Smith, B. (1985). Some home truths on the contemporary black feminist movement. *The Black Scholar, 16*(2), 4–13.

Smith, D. E. (2016). *Finding sanctuary in sisterhood: A middle school literacy group critically analyzes race, gender, and size* [Doctoral dissertation, University of South Carolina]. https://scholarcommons.sc.edu/etd/3960

Walker, A. (1989). *The temple of my familiar*. Mariner Books.

Waters, M., Evans-Winters, V. E., & Love, B. L. (2019). *Celebrating twenty years of Black girlhood: The Lauryn Hill reader*. Peter Lang.

CHAPTER 2

RE)MEMBERING LESSONS ON *DAUGHTERING*

A Black Woman's Journey Towards Healing, Love, and Self-Actualization During Health and Racial Pandemics

Amber Jean-Marie Pabon

This chapter examines my participation in a Black women's virtual litera-ture circle during an ongoing global health pandemic and racial crisis in the United States. The circle functioned as a protective factor, enabling me to survive and thrive as an early career scholar, mother, and daughter facing personal and professional challenges. Grounded in critical race fem-inism, I employ autoethnographic methods to examine how engagement with Black womanist-centered texts afforded opportunities for healing and developing mindful practices. Furthermore, I explicate how the circle revitalized my mental and spiritual well-being, resurrected my intellec-tual curiosity, and reinvigorated my scholarly agenda from the depths of professional burnout. I conclude with lessons learned for sustaining and extending wellness beyond the literature circle as a daughter, sister, and mother.

Introduction: Writing to Save My Backside

Throughout the process of writing this chapter across dual pandemics, my energy levels have fluctuated between periods of high-level productivity

Black Women Mothering & Daughtering During a Dual Pandemic:
Writing Our Backs, pp. 11–24
Copyright © 2024 by Information Age Publishing
www.infoagepub.com

and absolute stagnation. As articulated in the introduction, I am among many Black women attempting to thrive in the context of relentless raced and gendered oppression—an exponentially fatiguing ambition in a global health crisis. However, the opportunity to consistently reconceptualize Black women's mental health and labor during the dual pandemics is vivifying. The sisterhood that blossomed through our literacy circle was and is integral to striving, resisting, coping, and adapting in a macrosystem that devours our souls. I am honored to contribute to an unapologetically Black feminist book that articulates our herstories of critical reading, reflecting, and discussing Black women's literary scholarship.

A significant outcome of my participation in the Black woman's literacy circle has been a growing capacity to engage in critical self-reflection. This reflective capacity has enabled me to understand better the connections between my personal history, everyday struggles, professional accomplishments, and aspirations and situate this narrative alongside those of my ancestors and other Black women engaged in the collective struggle for humanity in the context of patriarchal white supremacy. My perspective on academic writing has shifted from consistently feeling like an imposter to writing to save my backside.

I'm a Recovering Undercover Under-Writer

My imposter syndrome struggles began when I started my first full-time academic position. Despite having climbed a career ladder from urban public school English teacher to literacy staff developer to Assistant Professor (now associate) of urban education as a single mom, I could not operationalize my resilience to navigate academia successfully, or more specifically, predominantly White institutions (PWIs) of higher learning. I had expected a space where ideas were valued, thoughtful debate ensued, and mentorship supported new faculty. Moreover, everything about my interviewing and hiring experience, as well as public-facing institutional statements, conveyed commitment to inclusivity. Perhaps it was all too good to be true—a snake oil hustle that woos naïve, newly minted PhDs eager for employment with promises of financial stability, support, and success while simultaneously disguising the stench of patriarchal white supremacy.

I could recount the numerous, highly egregious, raced, and gendered institutional challenges I faced—many of which are well documented in the existing body of literature on Black women academics (Berry, 2018; Gutierrez y Muhs et al., 2012). A more generative contribution involves centering Black women's survival during enduring racial and health pandemics. Finally, I draw from Black feminist thought and critical race feminism to theorize the healing power of collectively reading and studying Black women's literature with other sistas.

For several years as an early career scholar, I failed to see the relationship between institutionalized oppression, toxic academic culture, and my capacity to persevere. This environment induced chronic stress that contributed to the decline of my physical, mental, and spiritual well-being. As my health declined, so did my performance.

Specifically, my scholarly productivity dwindled, and I became a reluctant writer who struggled with procrastination. I neglected to pursue ideas that mattered to me out of fear of rejection. I also experienced rejection when I conformed to perceived expectations. As a result, I could not find my voice. Crippled by the anxiety that muddled my thoughts and sapped my energy, I acquiesced to an underlying belief that I was an imposter in the academy and stopped writing altogether. I withdrew from public life because I was embarrassed by my inability to thrive professionally and personally, further evidencing my imposter status when, in reality, my failure to manage the chronic stress in my professional life catalyzed maladaptive coping strategies that only exacerbated the problem. The breaking point was a significant health scare in the months before the pandemic that forced me to prioritize my well-being. After several intense months of physical rehabilitation, reprogramming dietary and exercise practices, and trauma-informed cognitive therapy, I returned to academic life much healthier and better equipped to manage stress through adaptive coping strategies. I was excited to re-engage with writing from a growth mindset— the belief that I could produce critical, thoughtful, relevant scholarship and needed to hone my skills. With this perspective in mind, my outreach to Dr. Venus Evans-Winters, also known as Dr. V, proved propitious as she was launching a Black women's literature circle. During Sunday afternoon virtual meetings across one year, we read literacy works by and about Black women. These meetings were for us, by us.

(Re)learning How to Research

Our initial reading, *Black Feminism in Qualitative Inquiry* (Evans-Winters, 2019), was kismet, personally and professionally. Collective reading and journaling inspired us to imagine, design, and engage critical research firmly grounded in Black womanish aesthetics. Furthermore, the text offered a methodological blueprint for Black women researchers to examine their data in myriad authentic forms.

Before that first Sunday afternoon meeting arrived, I was already deep into the book, having underlined several parts of the text and adhered post-its with my notes about personal, textual, and world connections on selected pages. Dr. V's initial words compelled me to reflect upon the limitations of White-centered training as a qualitative researcher. She wrote: "What does inscribed freedom look like in the data analysis process? Conversations with ancestors, deliberations with elders, rituals, ceremony, rites of passage, youth-centered pedagogy, and even the rejection of Eurocentric western notions of time and space" (Evans-Winters, 2019, p. 9).

How poignant! I have long struggled with tensions of representation in the process of writing about Black education. Capturing the languaging and sense-making of Black teachers and youth whom I have interviewed—and these interviews consistently sound and feel more like conversations than traditional question/answer sessions—using the expected conventions of academic research and writing has always presented challenges relative to authenticity and voice. My ears heard their brilliant nuance, and my heart felt their passionate engagement. Still, my head and hand frequently stumbled at communicating how I understand perspectives conveyed by Black educational stakeholders. In other words, I could design research in normative frameworks and engage in *dope-ass* ciphers with Black students, teachers, and school leaders, but I could not write to save my damn back. There was a mismatch between my colonized training in qualitative methods and the Black womanish ways I interpreted the counter-narratives of Black folks who shared their time and words with me. Evans-Winters (2019) identifies this paradox by stating:

> As long as we choose to play within the confines of Western Institutions and with an adopted language (i.e., academic English), Black women will always compromise, negotiate, and balance the needs of institutions and our struggles for social, economic, political, and education liberation. (p. 13)

Word up! The master's tools will never dismantle the master's house (Lorde, 1984, p. 2). What is so powerful about this excerpt is the succinct explanation of a moral dilemma that particularly marginalizes Black women academics. Our financial contracts with these institutions of higher learning are not without consequence. So, regardless of commitments to social justice or racial equity, should we wish to maintain employment and upward mobility, far too often, we conform to normative constructs that define the research and publication industry, among other aspects of our work. Navigating the contradictions of being true to our people in qualitative inquiry and simultaneously conforming to standardized research conventions etches away at the soul. In the absence of alternative sources of support, criticisms like "your research is not sufficiently rigorous, generalizable, or impactful" engender spirit murder that chisels the soul. However, the text's acknowledgment of the oppressive nature of dominant methodologies, alongside the discussion of Black feminist modalities for data collection and analysis, affirmed my qualms and liberated my thinking.

Pedagogy and Politicking

The concepts *of politicking*, *cultural reflections*, and *motherspeak* offer Black-centered analytical frames. Politicking creates space to link participants' authentic experiences to the larger sociopolitical contexts surrounding their lives. In reading Fieldnote Six, which provides an example of politicking, I immediately connected to the institutional context surrounding the relationship between Dr. V, the student worker, Nanette, and the narrative accounts. Dr. V's description of her initial encounter with Nanette is similar to my first-time meeting Dominique, an undergraduate student in my education foundations course. Dominque was the only Black female student in the class, and at that time, I was the only Black female faculty member in my department. Throughout the course, Dominique was highly engaged in lectures and discussions. She asked poignant questions, shared about her K–12 experiences, and challenged assumptions that often emerged among some of her white peers. I was often impressed and delighted by her insights, and when I was especially passionate, Dominque would co-sign through non-verbal cues that affirmed my praxis.

When I teach, I frequently draw from my prior experiences as a secondary English teacher, current sociopolitical issues, hip-hop music, and social media. I blend standardized English and Black cultural aesthetics to connect course concepts with critical issues related to racial bias, socioeconomic inequality, and gender oppression. This practice, rooted in Black feminist approaches to teaching, is, in part, a reflection of my authentic self and a model of culturally affirming pedagogy. I want students to understand teaching as a political act that necessitates preparation in methods and through studying and critiquing historical and contemporary issues. Furthermore, by utilizing my standpoint to foster community, I make explicit the importance of honoring multiple identities, demonstrating vulnerability, and engaging in an ethic of care.

Sometimes, however, my ambitions can be lost on White students. Code-switching to share narratives connecting course material to macro, meso, and micro-level phenomena fell flat because White students needed further explanation to make sense of the reference. In those moments, when I felt that hot, tingly sensation of embarrassment rising from the pit of my stomach, I would scan the room of blank stares in search of any indication that my words resonated with students. Frequently, Dominique seemed to recognize my probe, and she would meet my eyes to either nod her head in affirmation or furrow her brow quizzically, indicating the need to clarify.

Like me, Dominique emotes with her facial expressions, and seeing her eyes widen and her lips pursed as she processed my words and then posed thoughtful commentary filled my heart with joy. In other instances, when White students interjected before I finished speaking or demonstrated their ennui through loud yawns and slouching all over their chairs, Dominique remained on point, always remembering her home training. There was an understanding of Black cultural norms in the classroom—including paying attention when spoken to and demonstrating interest and respect in the body—that never required verbal explanation. As Evans-Winters (2019) writes:

> I believe for some Black women professors, we have high expectations of Black students, especially other Black women college students, in that they are to remain committed to an authentic Black identity and, as part of that identity, present a confident Black scholar identity. (p. 89)

Indeed, Dominique's critical questioning of the troubling history of public education and reflections on current issues that impact Black students demonstrated her intellectual curiosity. Her engagement and written assignments demonstrated her brilliance, but it was Dom's signifying (Smitherman, 1977) in class that let me know she was *down by law*—a term we used growing up in LA to describe a person who has your back. This young Black woman's presence demonstrated the power of connection grounded in Black womanness. Dominique disrupted feelings of insecurity and frustration by affirming that I made sense and was valued, and my supposition that I positively influenced her was confirmed later that semester. At our final class meeting, Dominique approached me after class and asked me to take a selfie with her. She shared that she had never had a Black woman teacher before and appreciated me and my teaching. When Dom talked about her aspirations to become a social studies teacher, I was reminded of myself when I entered the field of education, reaching out to Black elder teachers at a middle school in Bedford-Stuyvesant, Brooklyn, to learn from them. The feeling was sublime. She gave me so much hope for the next generation of Black teachers. In that cultural exchange (Evans-Winters, 2019) outside my classroom, similar to Dr. V and Nanette, the bond between Dominique and I was solidified.

We continued to stay in touch after the course ended, and when I established my program to support the pipeline of Black and Brown teachers, I hired Dominique as a student worker. We decided together that we did not like that name, so we called her role *student liaison*. Like Nanette, Dominque was the first Black student hired in that role in our department. She helped me build the program and was instrumental in the recruitment efforts at local high schools. Dominique also organized resources and events for current Black, Indigenous, People of Color students in the College of Education. Throughout the past few years, I have continued to reach out to Dom to gauge her perspective on important decisions. She reciprocates by asking thoughtful questions and sharing insights on institutional politics and policies. In addition, I have helped Dominique navigate predominantly White spaces in ways I wish someone had done for me as an undergraduate by keeping it real.

Looking back now, I realize Dominique had been checking me out to see "if I was a real down sister" (Evans-Winters, 2019, p. 89) from day one. Her texts posing questions or sharing comments were atypical of traditional professor-student relationships. In that space, we were Black and free, conversing about various topics relevant to Dom's personal and professional life as an emerging educator. The excerpt from a text message thread below (that she reviewed and approved for publication) reflects our typical politicking about teaching, capitalism, racism, and police brutality.

Pabon: Dom, how you doin?

Dom: It's alright not bad. How about yours?

Hopefully I can start working soon cause a sister is broke!

There's a Beverly Tatum quote that I'm not understanding. Can you explain?

Pabon: Lol, I'm gonna add you and your friends into my think tank!

Google Franz Fanon. He talks about resisting oppression and our complicity in the oppression of others. Also, Freire.

Dom: For real? I'm over here like…

*sends an image of Tupac in deep thought

Pabon: You wear Nikes? You got an iPhone? You shop at Walmart? Well, you/we are oppressed as Black folks and also engaged in the oppression of people living in poverty.

Dom: I feel like students don't even utilize the library all like that cause they're so into their phones

Pabon: Social media will not help you become a teacher. It's a starting place, but don't stay there (shoutout to Milner!)

Dom: I'm about to read Bettina Love next

Pabon: Yes, love to hear this!

Dom: Pabon, you seen them Trump signs by campus? A mess!

Pabon: I'm sorry. I was a little younger than you when Rodney King was beat, and the city of Los Angeles was defending the cops. Over 30 years later and things ain't changed.

For this author, the significance of Evans-Winters Fieldnote Six extends beyond the uncanny similarities between the two Black woman scholar-student relationships. As a researcher, the text permitted me to write our story for a publication that would have otherwise remained housed in our phones and memories. Concepts like cultural exchange, sistering, and daughtering helped me frame the narrative of the uniquely beautiful connections between Dominique and me, a story still being written as she enters her second year of teaching. Through reading and discussing Black feminism in qualitative inquiry, I saw myself and my experiences validated and valued, strengthened my sense of self. I re-imagined a Black woman scholarly identity that aligned my identities as a mother and daughter with the researcher and teacher.

For Charlie, Hazel, Kay, and Chloe

The concept of daughtering advanced in *Black Feminism Qualitative Inquiry* speaks to Black women's socialization, critical thinking, storytelling, coping with hatred, knowledge production, spirituality, imagination, and creativity. Evans-Winters (2019) begins the chapter by describing a ritual process for Black women towards engaging daughtering as a methodology that starts with practices such as acknowledging the ancestors at night, walking, breathing with intentionality, and daily journaling. As we entered the start of the pandemic, these rituals became integral to my physical well-being and mental health, but I was unprepared for the flood of memories that began to stir. I would look out my window, write and listen to a robin singing on a tree, and be reminded of my 5-year-old self sitting in monkey grass at the park with my mom, eating animal crackers. Alternatively, I would be on my daily hike at dawn, see a family of deer, and recall road trips across the country in my grandparents' brown Chrysler, sliding across the white leather backseat in the days before wearing seat belts was enforced. As memories flooded my mind, I continued to journal anecdotes from my childhood. I would call my mom or her cousin to fill in parts of stories I had forgotten or explain events behind photographs in our family albums. I added these details to my entries. Then, at our literature circle meetings, I felt affirmed when we discussed how the rituals impacted our thinking. Finally, a sacred space in which we were neither ashamed nor dissuaded from remembering that "we were daughters before we were women" (Evans-Winters, 2019, p. 138).

As we entered the first summer of the pandemic with continued mass death, business closures, and increased state-sanctioned terrorism on Black folks, I turned away from the chaos. I immersed myself in daily meditation on my identities as a daughter and mother. Evans-Winters (2019) coined "mother speak" to describe the "internal voice ... derived from socialization, formal learning, and biological instinct" (p. 94). I was compelled to listen deeply to the wisdom of my ancestors alongside my common sense will-to-survive and the necessity of continuing to make professional progress in codifying my collection of journal entries into formal writing. I began to examine the oral stories (now written) and photographs along with other primary source documents my mother had sent me across time, like her and my grandmother's K–12 report cards, my grandparents' love letters, and recipes. I am not an artist by any means, but after yet another literature circle discussion in which we were encouraged to tap into our creativity, I created my interpretation of our family tree out of newspaper, photographs, and terms I was meditating on during my research process. I hung the image on my wall as a muse to inspire my analysis of our family history.

One morning, after a long hike, I realized that relevant primary source documents about my family might also be reflected in public records, so I began searching an archival digital database. There, I found a trove of state-sponsored documents like census records, birth and death certificates, and military commendations that informed family member's life histories. At that moment, I was overcome by emotion at seeing my family members' life histories reflected in the data. In *Help Me to Find My People: The African American Search for Family Lost In Slavery*, Heather Williams (2012) speaks to this contemporary Black genealogical experience by writing:

> As contemporary African Americans pore over dusty government records in archives and troll internet sites to pull out and reclaim traces of obscured family members, they want to have a record of their ancestor's existence, a record that can be found in censuses, in regimental records, and in other documents that identify and confirm the existence of people who, for them, have previously existed only in family memory. These searchers want something more concrete than family-generated oral histories; they want documents that have more currency in a world that puts stock in paper and in written words.... It is a way of honoring the memory of people are rarely part of any scholarly history.... By unearthing ancestors, they also document their own history, establish their own extended past, and establish a place for themselves. (p. 198)

I first read these words years ago while working on my dissertation on the life histories of Black male teachers, perhaps the last time I experienced intense joy and affirmation about my writing. Returning to that methodology a decade later to better understand my life history was unexpected and inspiring. I crafted interconnected narratives about my great-great-great grandmother Rose, my great-grandmother Charlie, and her daughter Hazel from my lens as their granddaughter. The following excerpt on my grandmother Hazel is an example.

Curls That Last Past Dark

My earliest memories of learning how to be a daughter began in my grandmother Hazel's beauty shop in the 80s in South Central. As a young girl, I'd spend my weekends and school breaks with my gramma. She owned a beauty salon, and we'd awaken early to get ready for the day. She'd make a pot of grits, bacon, and white toast with peach jelly, and then we'd roll to the shop in her beige Cadillac (see Figure 3.2).

Figure 2.1

Gramma Hazel

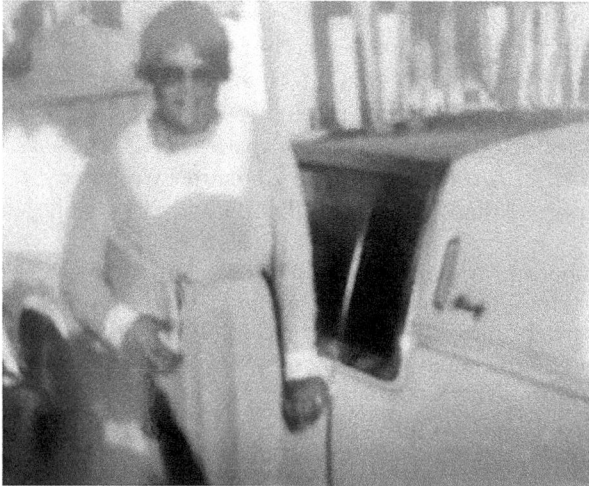

Smith's Beauty Shop was consistently packed with Black women of all ages wait-ing for her famous press and curls. She'd greet each client lovingly and always remembered the details they shared about their well-being, families, and careers. In the morning, the Channel Seven news would be playing, then the stories, followed by The People's Court, then back to the news. The small television had the worst reception, and she'd ask me to bang the top to stop the static. Shop talk frequently revolved around current local and world events, Angie and Jessie, and the coming and going of children and grandchildren.

We loved Hazel's shampoos with a touch of Sea Breeze for the scalp. She'd scoop thick gobs of Queen Helen's Cholesterol conditioner and saturate our thick hair from root to tip. Gramma sectioned the hair in quadrants and gently twisted it into knots that stayed in place. Even though more junior stylists used hand-held dryers with combs, she still used the old-school standing metal dryers with the long hose, manipulating the nozzle while combing each section. She'd finish off with a press and curl that lasted for two weeks. *Her clients were appreciative because when they got their hair done elsewhere, their curls wouldn't last till dark. My gramma kept her prices affordable (25 dollars for a wash/blow/press), and those ladies remained loyal for years.*

Throughout my years at the shop with my gramma, my role shifted from a passive observer absorbing all the talk and running back and forth to the bodega next door for snacks to shampoo girl. I practiced on "the head" (my grandmother's mannequin) and perfected the wet set, her favorite hairstyle. Eventually, my gramma let me do her hair, my great-aunt Marie's hair, and a few paying, tolerant customers who had known me since birth.

Hazel would drop knowledge at Smith's Beauty Shop, often politicking on the crack cocaine epidemic and gang violence going on right outside, but never from a deficit framework. She was well known by the neighborhood Crips, who seemingly looked out for her. When the cops who beat Rodney King were acquitted, and the store owner who killed Latasha Harlins was sentenced to only five years' probation, community service, and a $500 fine, a long stretch of Figueroa Boulevard succumbed to righteous uprising that destroyed many businesses. Her beauty shop was spared. The word on the street was that gang leaders ordered folks to stand down and several Black-owned businesses were untouched, contrary to news reports suggesting otherwise. Hazel loved her community, and the people loved her back from the 1950s until her retirement in the 90s (see Figure 2.2).

Figure 2.2

African American Women's Beauty Salon

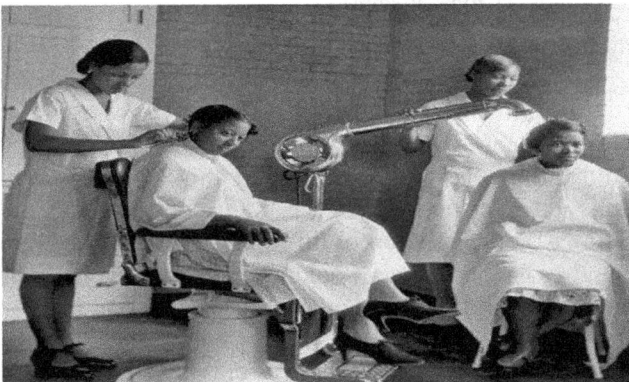

The process of remembering, reassembling, and reconnecting the pieces of my women ancestor's histories was a direct outcome of our literature circle's study of daughtering. Furthermore, engaging in this project created the conditions for critical self-reflection of my explicit and implicit socialization around my role as a daughter. As I re-read the narratives, I'd re-constructed to write this chapter, over and over, I was reminded of Evans-Winters's (2022) words, "We learn to be daughters through deliberate but keen observation, and at times, direct command.... As daughters, we learn early to serve" (p. 138). I began to understand how these lessons about how to be a Black girl were informed by their own experiences with love, pain, joy, fear, memory, knowledge-production, and spiritualism and that I had, for better or worse, been living out these instructions in relation to my mother Kay and in commune with my daughter Chloe. I could see anew the parts of myself I cherished and those aspects of self that seemed to originate from trauma. As we entered the warm season, I continued to meditate on the question, "How does engagement with inquiry and data serve my family, my communities, my self-worth, and the person I want to become?" (Evans-Winters, 2022, p. 139). I committed to the ongoing journey of self-actualization through a reckoning with how the past has shaped my identities as daughter/sister/mother/scholar. It was complex emotional labor and at times, I had more questions than answers.

Perhaps my maternal ancestors, Rose, Charlie, and Hazel, were preparing me to receive the wisdom that emerged through this inquiry. With making self-adjustments to better align a worldview grounded in valuing Black women's lived experiences, privileging our dialogues, enacting an ethic of care, and taking personal accountability (Hill-Collins, 2000) in words and deeds, came lucidity surrounding my life's purpose:

> I *am* my ancestor's wildest dreams.
>
> I *am* here to live out dreams deferred.
>
> I *am* keeper of Black folks' memories.
>
> I am teller of our stories.

For this Black girl, the second cold season of the dual pandemic was marked by inner peace. Despite ongoing pandemic turmoil over masks, vaccines, and variants, as well as continued anti-Black, anti-women, and anti-gay/trans state-sanctioned violence, I felt poised and focused on my goals, including the completion of this manuscript. However, the ancestors had another lesson for me. Looking back, I believe I was alerted of something awry through a brief but serious illness that forced me to pay closer attention to my body's signals. I returned to the daughtering rituals, refocusing on managing external stressors with clean eating, exercise, water, yoga, and rest. I was looking forward to winter break when I got the strangest text from my mom. The words made no sense. I kept texting back and calling to decipher what she was saying to no avail. Her health had drastically declined, and she'd been hospitalized. Somehow, we had one last conversation on a Saturday morning. "Everything's gonna be alright mom," I repeated until I heard her falling asleep. She passed peacefully a few days later, just before Christmas, at 66 years old (see Figure 2.2).

Figure 2.3

Kay and Amber

Similar to the outset of writing this chapter, I struggled with conclud- ing. But this time, it was not because I felt like an imposter who did not rightfully belong in academic spaces. Quite differently, this time, because I had given myself permission to write about some *real-life shit* (my data) and employed lessons from daughtering (methodology) to help me examine and convey these truths (discussion), I was imbued with *spirit energy* (Evans- Winters, 2022, p. 140) relative to the significance of this project. While I wish my mother were still here, I have so much gratitude for Dr. V and for the community of Black women by my side in the process.

Participating in the Black women's literature circle and developing a Black-women-centered genealogical tool throughout the dual pandemics that I was able to take up to craft her obituary. I am hopeful that other academic sistas and daughters might find the experiences, reflections, imaginings, and knowledge-outcomes described in this chapter generative for writing their backs toward healing, joy, and liberation.

REFERENCES

Berry, T. (2018). *From oppression to grace: Women of color and their dilemmas within the academy*. Stylus.

Collins, P. (2000). *Black feminist thought: Knowledge, consciousness and the politics of empowerment*. Hyman.

Evans-Winters, V. (2019). *Black feminism in qualitative inquiry*. Routledge.

Gutierrez, M. G., Niemann, Y. F., Gonzalez, C. G., & Harris, A. P. (Eds.). (2012). *Presumed incompetent: The intersections of race and class for women in academia*. Utah State University Press.

Lorde, A. (1984). *Sister outsider: Essays and speeches*. Crossing Press.

Smitherman, G. (1977). *Talkin and testimony: The language of Black America*. Wayne State University Press.

Williams, H. A. (2012). *Help me to find my people: The African American search for family lost in slavery*. University of North Carolina Press.

CHAPTER 3

WHEN THE FAMILY CRIES FOR HELP

Serving Community by Creating a S.T.E.M Sanctuary

Theresa Y. Robinson

Black women like Nannie Helen Burrough, Mary McCleod Bethune, and Marva Collins used teaching as an act of resistance to inequitable education systems for Black children. The dual pandemics of the COVID-19 virus and American racial injustice drew attention to the lack of equity in STEM education that Black families receive. The purpose of this chapter is to explain how a literature circle focused on Black women's mental health was simultaneously used as a healing space and source of empowerment for the author's experiences teaching and organizing STEM education for Black youth and families during the pandemics. The STEM Learning Series was developed to (1) provide hands-on, inquiry-based STEM education for conceptual understanding and (2) center the Black child, their social and emotional well-being, language, histories, and genius. The chapter offers reflections on how activism served to empower families during the pandemic (and be empowered by) those whom the author served.

When we went into lockdown for the COVID-19 health pandemic, I received calls from friends asking, "I do not understand this new math! What should I do?" I listened as mothers expressed concern about the lack of science teaching during online learning. I read social media posts from frustrated parents about their perceived lack

Black Women Mothering & Daughtering During a Dual Pandemic:
Writing Our Backs, pp. 25–39
Copyright © 2024 by Information Age Publishing
www.infoagepub.com
All rights of reproduction in any form reserved.

of ability to help their children with science and math schoolwork. I listened to reports from teacher friends about parents who were forced to leave their children home alone to engage in e-learning while they worked in the newly created category of essential workers. I felt their frustration, anxiety, and fatigue. I heard their cry and felt compelled to help. I decided I could be of service to my community. I organized my colleagues and a middle grades math education student to teach science and math subjects online to families free of cost during the pandemic. We provided hands-on STEM experiences that centered the Black child's cultural funds of knowledge. As I wrote this piece, I struggled with the title. The original title was STEM for Cultural Sustainability: A Pedagogy of Activism. That title felt sterile to me. The words and phrases dismantling, disrupting, "I cannot help my child," and sanctuary space resonated with me. I knew this was not just about e-learning during the pandemic. The title of this piece reflects what I did when I heard families cry out for help with math and science learning as they were either working from home or serving as essential workers during the dual pandemics of COVID-19 and racial injustice.

The purpose of this chapter is to explain how a literature circle focused on Black women's mental wealth was simultaneously used as a healing space and source of empowerment for the author's experiences teaching and organizing science and math education for Black youth and families during the pandemics. In addition, the chapter offers reflections on the author's experience as a Black woman in STEM and ways in which activism served to empower families during the pandemics (and be empowered by) those who were served. The contributions of African Americans and women to the advancement of STEM (science, technology, engineering, and mathematics) have historically been erased from K–12 public education. The contributions of African Americans and women to the advancement of STEM has historically been erased from K–12 public education curriculum and subsequently instruction. The erasure of the contributions of Black women to scientific enterprise has adversely impacted the representation and participation of Black women in STEM fields of study and the workforce. Additionally, the population of STEM teachers is less diverse than the students they serve. While the percentage of students of color has increased from 46% to 52% over the last decade, teachers of color have remained at 15% (Illinois State Board of Education [ISBE], 2018). This discrepancy leads to classrooms in which STEM teachers may not recognize or respect the unique cultural backgrounds of their students. Students do not enter the classroom as empty vessels waiting to be filled by their teachers. Students bring rich cultural experiences from home life with them to the classroom. Moll et al. (1992) refer to these cultural experiences as funds of knowledge that may be used by teachers to access students' prior knowledge. The knowledge and information teachers present are filtered through the child's unique cultural worldview. Failure to recognize this reality may diminish student engagement in the STEM fields (National Research Council [NRC], 2012).

In the tradition of educators like Nannie Helen Burroughs, Mary McCleod Bethune, and Marva Collins, teaching was exercised as activism, utilized as resistance to inequitable education experiences for Black children during the COVID-19 pandemic. Teaching and advocacy were grounded in Black women's literary works, culturally relevant and sustaining pedagogical theory, and best practices in science and math teaching and learning. Activism served to remedy Black families adversely impacted by the pandemics by (1) providing hands-on, inquiry-based science and math education for conceptual understanding, (2) centering the Black child, their social and emotional well-being, language, histories, and genius, and (3) integrating language and literacies in science and math teaching and student learning.

CULTURALLY RELEVANT PEDAGOGY

The dual pandemics of the COVID-19 virus and American racial injustice drew attention to the inadequate STEM education Black children and families receive. Using culturally relevant pedagogy, best practices in STEM education, and Black feminist thought, my scholarship and activism centered on articulating resistance to the status quo of unsatisfactory STEM education for Black children and families. In her seminal research with successful teachers of Black students, Ladson-Billings (1994) put forth the philosophy of culturally relevant pedagogy (CRP). The three tenets of CRP revolutionized approaches to curriculum and instruction for Black students and, subsequently, all marginalized students, asserting that (1) students must experience academic success, (2) students must develop and/ or maintain cultural competence, and (3) students must develop a critical consciousness to challenge the status quo to experience excellence in their education experience. Paris (2012) built upon CRP by positing that culturally sustaining pedagogy (CSP) must seek to perpetuate, foster—sustain linguistic, literate, and cultural pluralism as part of the democratic project of schooling (p. 93). CSP includes the importance of language and literacy in discussions around culturally relevant pedagogy. The unique home and social language children bring to the classroom should be honored and used as a foundation for the development of academic language. As a Black woman, scientist, and educator, my role is ensuring the valuing and inclusion of contributions of Black scientists, engineers, and mathematicians, as well as Black teachers' and students' voices, as a vital role in STEM education. In addition to culturally relevant, the term culturally sustaining is used here because it requires educators to support communities in sustaining the cultural and linguistic competencies while simultaneously offering access to dominant cultural competence (p. 95).

CULTURALLY RELEVANT STEM EDUCATION

Due to the increasing demand for science-related, problem-solving-oriented professions and technological advancements, educators must prepare Black students for success in an ever- changing world. Students need development as creative and critical thinkers to ask questions and design solutions. While it is recognized that not every child will become a scientist, engineer, or mathematician, our responsibility is to teach all students in STEM classrooms the science concepts and engineering practices that will prepare them to address the issues they will face in their everyday lives. STEM education focusing on developing scientifically and mathematically literate students will create a STEM literate populace. STEM literacy helps students understand why we should reuse glass jars rather than throw them in the garbage, why they should not flush unused prescription medications down the drain, how to mentally calculate a 10% discount on an item for purchase, and when shooting a basketball why one needs to put a little arc in the release. STEM literacy helps students understand why wearing a mask during an airborne virus outbreak is primarily a matter of science rather than politics. It is these everyday experiences with STEM in the world around us that make literacy an essential outcome for science and math education. Science and math literacy is more than memorization of facts but rather the ability to ask questions, think critically, interpret data, and make conclusions based on data and gathered evidence (NRC, 1996, 2012). The Framework for K–12 Science Education and Next Generation Science Standards (NGSS), requires a shift in teaching and learning practices that includes inquiry-based teaching models. Inquiry requires students to participate in scientific and engineering practices (SEP) via eight SEPs:

1. Asking questions (for science) and defining problems (for engineering).
2. Developing and using models.
3. Planning and carrying out investigations.
4. Analyzing and interpreting data.
5. Using mathematics and computational thinking.
6. Constructing explanations (for science) and designing solutions (for engineering.
7. Engaging in argument from evidence; and
8. Obtaining, evaluating, and communicating information (NRC, 2012, p. 49).

The implementation of the NGSS has changed the way educators teach and how students experience science across American K–12 public schools. Accordingly, the most effective way to teach *STEM for All* learners should be coupled with culturally relevant and sustaining practices. Building on the tenets of CRP, CSP, and best practices for science education, I used the SALK framework for organizing teacher training and curriculum and instruction during the pandemic. The SALK model for culturally relevant STEM education is grounded in the conceptual frameworks of culturally relevant and sustaining pedagogies (Ladson-Billings, 1994; Paris, 2012), components of universal design for learning, academic language development, and strategies for content area literacy. The framework also draws upon the recommendations for diversity and equity in science education of the Framework for K–12 Science Education (NRC, 2012). The SALK model provides a framework by which educators can plan for culturally relevant STEM curricula and instruction. The framework is based on four components:

- **STEM as a cultural accomplishment**—integrate the social study of STEM as a means to support the positive racial, ethnic, and linguistic identity of students. Studying the lives and triumphs of notable figures in STEM not only presents positive images but also provides representation and narratives of achievement.
- **Action and expression**—provide students with explicit methods and support to understand the
- "how" of learning. This guiding principle allows students to set personal learning goals.
- **Language and literacies**—use content area literacy strategies to teach STEM content. Understand language patterns as a foundation for the development of academic language. Explicitly teach and focus on STEM language form, function, and vocabulary.
- **Knowledge of students**—use approaches for getting to know students socially and emotionally, their cultural assets, and funds of knowledge as a foundation for curriculum and instruction.

The SALK model was used to train the teachers who would teach after-school online science and math classes for students during the pandemic. The STEM Learning Series was developed in response to family needs during e-learning at the height of the pandemic. The expressed goals were to center the Black child, their social and emotional well-being, and STEM learning during the pandemic(s). Parents and families were invited to explore how they could play a critical role in promoting students' high regard for themselves as learners of science and mathematics.

CULTURALLY RELEVANT STEM METHODOLOGY

Reflective narrative, theoretical and practical knowledge were used to discuss how the Black women's literature circle and teaching were used as activism during the pandemics. An invitation to join the Black Women's Mental Wealth Group during the pandemics of the COVID-19 virus, anti-Blackness and white supremacy, provided a space for reflection on my experiences as a Black woman in STEM. It also offered a space to imagine a solution to the lack of equity in STEM education Black children and families were receiving during the quarantine. The revolutionary act of centering Black women's mental health while reading, writing, and discussing the literary works of Black women awakened my sense of purpose as a scholar, activist, and educator. The group anchored me in my spiritual and cultural heritage as a Black daughter, granddaughter, sister, and mother. While reading during the literature circle, I was inspired by Morrison (2019) to resist, encouraged by Walker (1989) to dream, and empowered by by Evans-Winters (2019) to tell my story. I was empowered because her work went beyond the theoretical into the practical. Her groundbreaking text, *Black Feminism in Qualitative Inquiry* (Evans-Winters, 2019) provided thoughts on how transgression in our lives as Black women could be used to tell the story scientifically. I could see how these works reflected my lived experiences as a scholar and activist. Evans-Winters gave a heart to science. For example, she writes, "Black women will always compromise, negotiate, and balance the needs of institutions and our struggle for social, economic, and education liberation" (p. 13). She goes on to comment, "Black women's worldview is shaped by our everyday joys and struggles as well as our quests to solve our community's problems and pushback against societal barriers" (p. 15). I heard my community cry out for help and I felt compelled to find solutions to the barriers of inadequate and unequal STEM education. Reading the literary works of Black women within a sisterhood served as a means of coping with the health pandemic and the outrage associated with state-sanctioned violence against Black people. One of the tenets of Black feminist thought is the commitment to challenging racism, and sexism is rooted in their lived experiences. My experiences with racism and sexism as a biology student and future educator bear witness to Black feminist theory in action.

Being a Black Woman in STEM

I graduated from a state-supported university with a Bachelor of Science in Biological Sciences and Secondary Education. The university was situated in a rural community surrounded by national forests spotted with prehistoric flora and fauna. Historically, the area is known as a slave-holding community within a free state referred to as "Little Egypt." The university is situated on land inhabited by forcibly removed and murdered indigenous Native Americans.

> The earliest written accounts of the Illinois Indians, ca. 1639, authoritatively specify they occupied lands bounded by the Wisconsin, Ohio, Wabash, and Mississippi Rivers in 60 villages with over 20,000 men or warriors. The Illinois called themselves "Inoca" while French explorers and missionaries generally referred to them as "Illinois." There may have been as many as 12 different Illinois tribes; however, by the end of the century, seven of these tribes—including the Chepoussa, Chinkoa, Coiracoentanon, Espeminkia, Maroa, Moingwena, and Tapouaro—had disappeared or merged with other Illinois tribes. Five principal tribes survived into the 1700s: the Cahokia, Kaskaskia, Michigamea, Peoria, and Tamaroa. Only the Kaskaskia and Peoria continued to exist in the early 1800s. (USDA Forest Service, 2022)

Within these contexts, I was a social, political, and racial minority. Sometimes, I was the only Black student in my science classes, the only woman, and more frequently, the only Black woman. Before I knew what intersectionality was, I was living the experience. It had become familiar practice not to be chosen or chosen last as a lab partner. I was challenged to achieve and excel as a Black woman in a STEM major with very little collegial support. What I lacked in institutional support was made up for in communal support. After earning grades of C in significant science and math classes, I was arrogant enough to believe that the professors were not teaching correctly. My next move changed the course of my career path. I perused the course catalog and found an introduction to teaching class. My goal was to learn what "good teaching" looked like and subsequently be able to challenge the pedagogical choices of my science and math professors with research-based evidence. During the class, we read Johnathon Kozol's (1991) *Savage Inequalities*. The text illuminated that inequalities in schooling for racial minorities were a systemic problem rather than a local issue. Chapter 2 of *Savage Inequalities*, "Other People's Children: North Lawndale and the South Side of Chicago," reflected my experience growing up and attending school on the south side of Chicago. After reading the text and conversing with the professor, I added a second major, Secondary Education. Reading about the systemic differences in public education for minority students led to an epiphany that my purpose was to be a science educator instead of a laboratory scientist. My role would be to liberate children through STEM education.

My student teaching assignment was in a more rural community than the university. The only access to the town was a two-lane road. My cooperating teacher was a tall, skinny white man with a slow southern drawl.

Mr. Denver Tolbert was a former coal miner who had lost his job when the mines closed. He had a thick mustache that he twirled from time to time. Upon first meeting him, I knew in my heart that he was prejudiced. I had encountered many people who looked like him, but I soon realized I was projecting upon him the same preconceived notions many in education place upon Black children. While walking in the building on the first day of school, I suppose he could sense my trepidation because he said, "Don't worry, I'll tell you whom to stay clear of." This was an acknowledgment that (1) there were people in the building who held discriminatory and/or racist beliefs about Black people and (2) he was an ally. Two African American students in my class were siblings. There was one other African American adult in the building, and she served as a teaching assistant for the special education classroom in the basement level. I taught the traditional eighth-grade science curriculum, but I quickly learned the role of culturally relevant pedagogies. My classic science teacher education grounded in the philosophies and theories of John Dewey, Jean Piaget, and Jerome Bruner had yet to fully prepare me for this eventuality. I could draw upon my lived experiences as a Black girl from the southside of Chicago and Kozol's text to understand the context in which I was teaching. For example, no students were marked absent on the first day of hunting season, or the absence was excused if parents informed the school that the child went hunting. It was reminiscent of the agreement between the school and the family of Burris Ewell described in Harper Lee's (1960) *To Kill a Mockingbird*. The school community understood that the sustenance of many families depended on a successful hunting season. In their eight years of schooling, none of the students ever had a Black or female science teacher. Many had never visited Chicago, which was approximately 300 miles north. What they knew about Black life was from television and media. My identity as a Black woman from an urban area with expertise in science was a mystery to them. I learned first- hand the importance of drawing from students' funds of knowledge as described by (Moll et al., 1992) as an asset for curriculum and instruction instead of a deficit to be overcome. Teaching in a rural community provided me with an opportunity to understand the importance of culture and context in science teaching.

After completing student teaching, I accepted a position as a high school science teacher in Chicago Public Schools. Rather than culturally isolated, middle-level, white rural children, my student population was 100% African American ninth graders. Of the class, some were gifted and talented, while others were functionally illiterate. Two entered ninth grade as mothers, and a couple were required to report to their probation officer regularly. In both contexts of teaching and learning, rural and urban, I had to advocate for a science curriculum and instruction that was relevant to the culture and lives of my students. I covered topics like the base ten nature of the metric system until all students understood instead of moving on to the next topic. I knew that a solid foundation in the metric system would serve the student's future academic success in STEM. I asked students to write a question they had about the world around them. They used those questions to create science investigations and research papers. We studied the scientific endeavors and discoveries of Dr. Percy Julian, George Washington Carver, Dr. Mae Jemison, and Dr. Ben Carson (the story of his life and medical accomplishments before he became a part of the 45th President of the United States administration). It was in these early years of my career that I developed a pedagogy of activism for cultural sustainability in science education. Over 20 years after reading Kozol's *Savage Inequalities*, literature again would serve as motivation to take action against inequality in STEM education during the pandemics. Many were not aware of the second pandemic. The acts of violence against Black bodies and subsequent riots became evident. Anti-Blackness in America had come to a head. A pedagogy rooted in activism would be needed to address both.

DUELING PANDEMICS—EMOTIONS AND EVENTS

Racism was emerging in a way never seen since the pre-civil rights movement, causing a physical and psychological response for many Black Americans. Emotional experiences, partly from isolation due to the threat of illness and possible death due to the COVID-19 virus, became the second pandemic. The threat of COVID-19 and racial injustice became dueling pandemics for Black people. Between January 9 and 21, 2020, the World Health Organization and the Center for Disease Control (CDC) announced a mysterious coronavirus-related pneumonia in Wuhan, China, and the first confirmed U.S. case, respectively. While watching developments related to the COVID-19 virus internationally, on February 23, 2020, Ahmad Arbery, a 25-year-old, unarmed Black man was pursued while jogging and shot and killed by two white vigilantes in Georgia. It was not until March 13, 2020, that former President Donald Trump declared COVID-19 a national emergency. On the *same* day, March 13, 2020, 26-year-old Breonna Taylor's home was entered by plain-clothed officers of the Louisville, Kentucky Metropolitan Police Department while she slept and was fatally shot. A Black man was murdered while jogging, and a Black woman was murdered while sleeping in her home. As Black Americans, we were again reminded that we were vulnerable for simply existing. We were collectively contending with another string of 21st-century lynchings while a highly contagious, unknown, deadly virus swept the nation. When the COVID-19 pandemic hit American consciousness, public schools closed their doors to in-person learning, and many families were sent into a tailspin.

I was fielding text messages and online social media posts from friends and family about their frustrations with remote learning/homeschooling. Some were frustrated because they did not know how to help their child with this "new math." Others were struggling with having to work from home while teaching. My first way of helping was to create a video on social media from my work office space explaining and demonstrating how one can help their child with science and math using everyday items and experiences around the home. My goal was to reduce parent panic while empowering families to engage in a form of "homeschooling." I explained how everyday activities like cooking can help students understand the metric system, and playing with toys like race cars can support understanding basic physics principles. While parents and families were adjusting to remote learning/homeschooling, the penultimate act of violence towards Black bodies occurred on May 25, 2020. Mr. George Floyd was murdered while being arrested for allegedly using a counterfeit bill in Minneapolis, Minnesota. The murder was witnessed, video recorded by onlookers, and shared around the globe. The rest of the world was welcomed to join Black Americans in the horrors of the state-sanctioned murder of unarmed Black people. White America's collective conscience had been roused. The majority could no longer deny, dismiss, or minimize claims of racial injustice and the need for police reform. One of the most haunting parts of the George Floyd murder video, which I refused to view, was when 46-year-old Floyd called out for his mother. It was the call heard worldwide by Black mothers, especially those with Black sons. I asked myself, what more can I do to help my community?

A month before the murder of Mr. George Floyd, a national group, The Black Women's Mental Wealth Academy, was organized by the Planet Venus Institute to explore the kinds of cultural work that Black women engage in, including teaching and community advocacy. The group's organizer drew upon Black women's literary productions to help us cope with issues specific to Black women and families, especially during the pandemics. The selected texts centered on the lived experiences of Black women and girls. We read Winters-Evans's (2019) *Black Feminism in Qualitative Inquiry*, Alice Walker's (1989) *Temple of my Familiar*, Morrison's (2019) The *Source of Self-regard: Selected Essays, Speeches, and Meditations, and Thick: And Other Essays* (2019) by Tressie McMillan Cottom. The texts were chosen to help us explore how we have learned to strive, resist, adapt, and re-conceptualize our mental health and labor during the dual pandemics of white supremacy and COVID-19. The group read and met virtually to reflect critically on our teaching, mentoring, activism, and justice work. More importantly, we were able to use Black women's literature as a way to cope with the global health pandemic and racial unrest. During this time, I struggled to make sense of and help my child process the murders of Ahmaud Arbery, Breonna

Taylor, and George Floyd. Amid a global health crisis, Black people were experiencing the trauma of the murder of Black people on public display. I was experiencing this trauma while teaching methods and materials for teaching secondary science and seminars on communication and collaboration to future teachers. The sister reading circle became a place to breathe and exhale metaphorically.

A PEDAGOGY OF ACTIVISM

On racism and fascism, Morrison (2019) wrote, the genius of fascism is that any political structure can host the virus, and virtually any developed country can become a suitable home. Morrison's words foreshadowed the virus-like biological nature of racism and fascism, especially in America. Accordingly, labels like Democratic, Republican, liberal, conservative, right-wing, and left-wing alike can serve as the host for the racism and fascism virus. While many pundits spoke of ideologies, Morrison reminded us, fascism talks ideology, but it is just marketing for power.. Educational equity means every student has access to the educational resources and rigor they need at the right moment in their educational experience across race, ethnicity, and language. History and current trends indicate that many Black children are in schools that lack the resources they need to participate in high-quality education fully. The right moment for educational activism occurred during the 2020–2021 academic year. The pandemics drew attention to the lack of equity in public education, especially in STEM education for Black children and families. Children were in schools that lacked updated broadband Wi-Fi capability, teachers were not fully trained to teach with technology, and many families lacked the hardware and willingness to participate in remote learning. A pedagogy of activism was needed because, as Morrison (2019) warned, the move towards a final solution [racism & fascism] happens in steps that include criminalizing the enemy and then preparing, budgeting for, and rationalizing the building of holding arenas, especially for its men and absolutely its children, for many children schools represent those holding arenas. Remote learning was an opportunity to reconnect our children and families to their cultural heritage of excellence in science, technology, engineering, and mathematics. However, that was difficult for some families because the work-life/remote learning balance was a challenge for many families. A pedagogy of activism is one in which curriculum and pedagogical practices are grounded in students' historical, cultural, and everyday lives in support of educational justice. Enacting a pedagogy of activism in STEM education meant being collectively responsible for my sisters, brothers, cousins, and play-cousin's children.

I decided to use my passion and knowledge of science and education in the struggle for the liberation of our people. Outside institutions not historically designed to support our social and academic success, I would do this. In collaboration with two community-based organizations, three eight-week online science and math courses were designed and implemented for student's Grades K–8. The following is an example of how collaboration with community-based organizations around family STEM needs during the pandemics changed how students experience STEM instruction.

THE STEM LEARNING SERIES

Empowered by the texts we read in the Black Women's Mental Health Group, the STEM Learning Series was developed to support the many Black families who were essential workers, out of work, or working from home and desired support for their child's STEM learning. A middle-level mathematics education student was enlisted, Ms. Ashley O'Donnell, and a district- level K–9 Math Director, Ms. Oluwafunmilayo Ajayi, agreed to teach in the program. We met to plan the curriculum and review the SALK method as a foundation for instruction. The science and math courses included connections to students' cultural histories and big ideas in science and math. Centering the experiences of Black children to see themselves and their histories reflected in STEM curriculum and instruction revitalized my soul and served to empower families who were being served. It became a way to understand and resist patriarchy and racism during the health and racial pandemics. Working to make high-quality STEM accessible while increasing scientific and mathematical literacy in our communities became a way to resist the hegemony of racism and fascism and organize families and educators. Three courses were designed and developed in collaboration with the Black Educational Advocacy Coalition (BEAC) and Lions Club International for children and families; Black History Through Science for Grades 6–8, Mathematical Patterns in Nature for Grades K–2, and Math Games for Grades 5–8. Each family was mailed a STEM kit with supplies and materials. Curricular and instructional decisions were grounded in the SALK model. The following is a discussion of the curriculum and instruction plan with reflections from students and parents to demonstrate impact.

Course One: Black History Through Science Grades 6–8

Hands-on STEM activities were integrated with Black history for an eight-week course for students Grades 6–8. Concepts and principles of biology and chemistry were integrated with social studies. Each session of the class began with students completing a wellness check-in. The purpose of the check-in was to engage and activate their social-emotional learning. Students were asked to rate their emotional state using a smiley face Likert-type scale. On other days, they rated themselves using a meme of varied cat expressions. The course was divided into two sections: biological sciences and physical sciences. The biology portion of the course explored the concept of the basic unit of life, the cell. While it is customary for middle school students to learn the parts and functions of animal and plant cells in this class, a deep study of the cell membrane and nucleus was the focus. The purpose was for students to develop an understanding of the concept of selective permeability and the structure and function of the cell membrane, including the processes of diffusion and osmosis. The biology learning experiences included the diffusion and osmosis lab used to investigate the concept of selective permeability. These biological concepts were connected to the life of Henrietta Lacks. Students were able to make a connection between the harvesting of Mrs. Lack's cancer cells without the informed consent of the patient. A read-aloud strategy for introducing *The Immortal Life of Henrietta Lacks* (Skloot, 2011) was paired with a viewing of the Oprah Winfrey-produced movie of the same title. After learning about the cell and the life of Ms. Lacks during class, one student said, "They took her cells; that was not right what they did to her." Statements such as this are evidence students were beginning to connect science concepts to the real world. The physical science unit focused on the basic unit of matter, the atom. Students used Bohr Models to develop an understanding of the basic unit of matter—the atom—as the building blocks of molecules. The life, scientific endeavors, and discoveries of Dr. Percy L. Julian were read and written about as a connection to physical science concepts and Black history. Students investigated chemical reactions using household chemicals such as vinegar and hydrogen peroxide mixtures to measure temperature change as a function of a chemical reaction. When asked what made the course effective, one parent commented on the course evaluation, "The connection of learning STEM while also learning about Black Scientists."

Course Two: Mathematical Patterns in Nature for Grades K–2

From the petals of flowers to the migration of birds, mathematical patterns are everywhere. Over eight weeks, primary students developed observational skills in an integrated literacy, mathematics, and science unit of study. Through the lens of investigating plants and trees, students explored topics that include fractals, shapes, and symmetry. Chicago is steeped in rich history, and its grid system was the perfect playground for learning about mathematics. Social-emotional well-being was centered on the children in the class. Students were asked to rate their feelings at the beginning of each session with a smiley face Likert-type scale. One kindergarten student said, "It's fun; we get to do things." Students who participated in this class applied principles of patterns in mathematics through online and outdoor field experiences. While the class met online, there were two field days. On Halloween day, students and families met face to face at a park to create tree sketchings. Students were provided soil, seeds, a science journal, and other materials to observe and record observations of the growth of a seed. In a social media post about the culmination of the class, one parent wrote.

Course Three: Math Games for Grades 5–8

Mathematical reasoning and computation are used in our everyday lives. In this course, students explored mathematical concepts and how these concepts are used in board and dice games. The goal of the course was for students to understand concepts and explain the mathematical skills necessary to play a game, such as pattern recognition, probability, fractions, problem-solving, and strategic skills. Student objectives included (1) recognizing patterns, (2) understanding fractions probability, (3) learning strategies to play games, and (4) being able to explain the mathematical concepts behind a game. Throughout the course, students learned numbers and operations related to fractions, ratios and proportional relationships, probability, and how to reason abstractly and quantitatively. By the end of the course, students created a board game using the mathematical concepts learned. Students were encouraged to use creativity when making these games, but more importantly, when developing the rules for the game, explain the mathematical concepts needed to play. The purpose of this course was to integrate social-emotional learning, specifically self-awareness, in support of mathematical principles for everyday life. The course focused on incorporating board games, dice, and cards into math learning. This approach to mathematics can help reduce students' anxiety around mathematics and improve their attitudes and academic performance.

THE IMPACT OF CENTERING BLACK WOMEN'S MENTAL HEALTH

Black and Brown people were the majority of essential workers during the viral pandemic; we were simultaneously processing our collective racial trauma and supporting our children's learning. Continued exposure to violence and genocide of Black people while socially isolated was a significant issue concerning children's mental health. Many parents were making difficult decisions about whether to send their children back to school face to face and grappling with how to support their students' learning in online environments. The STEM Learning Series grew out of this need and was supported by the sisterhood literature circle that centered on Black women's mental health through literature. As a community organizer, I was able to reflect on my own educational experiences and create a vision for advancing of our culture through STEM education. The systemic impact of separating Black and African culture from STEM education disproportionately impacts Black students. I was reminded of my charge by the words of educator and activist Mary McLeod Bethune in a (1975) *Ebony* magazine article, "I leave you a thirst for education. Knowledge is the prime need of the hour, more and more.... If we continue in this trend, we will be able to rear increasing numbers of strong, purposeful men and women, equipped with vision, mental clarity, health, and education" (p. 47).

REFERENCES

Bethune, M. M. (1975). My last will and testament. *Ebony Magazine, 31*(1), 44–50.
    Evans-Winters, V. (2019). *Black feminism in qualitative inquiry*. Routledge.
Illinois State Board of Education (ISBE). (2018). *Unfilled Positions 2018*. https://www.
    isbe.net/unfilledpositions
Kozol, J. (1991). *Savage inequalities: Children in America's schools*. Crown.
Ladson- Billings, G. (1994). *The Dream Keepers: Successful teachers of African American
    Children*. Jossey-Bass.
Lee, H. (1960). *To kill a mockingbird*. HarperCollins.
Moll, L. C., Amanti, C., Neff, D., & Gonzalez, N. (1992). Funds of knowledge for
    teaching: Using a qualitative approach to connect homes and classrooms.
    Theory Into Practice, 31(2), 132–141.
Morrison, T. (2019). *Source of self-regard: Selected essays, speeches, and meditations*.
    Knopf Doubleday.
National Research Council. (1996). *The National Science Education Standards*.
    National Academy Press.
National Research Council. (2012). *A Framework for K–12 Science Education: Practices,
    crosscutting concepts, and core ideas:* The National Academies Press.
Paris, D. (2012). Culturally sustaining pedagogy: A needed change in stance, ter-
    minology, and practice. *Educational Researcher, 41*(3), 93–97.
Skloot, R. (2011). *The immortal life of Henrietta Lacks*. Random House.
USDA Forest Service. (2022, August 14). *Native American Heritage: Native tribes of
    Southern Illinois*. Retrieved August 14, 2022, from https://www.fs.usda.gov/
    detail/shawnee/home/
Walker, A. (1989). *Temple of my familiar*. Harcourt Brace Jovanovich.

CHAPTER 4

TOUTE BAGAI

Resistance and Reclaiming

Dyanis Conrad

This chapter explores the intersections of Black womanhood, sisterhood, and scholarship through the lens of endarkened and indigenous frameworks. I interrogate the ways in which my race, gender, and motherhood influence the content and context of my work and how a series of candid conversations with found sisters shaped personal and professional growth. This chapter symbolizes self-embrace and a roar of resistance to the oppressive nature of academia that seeks to reshape the Other in its image. This sister circle created space through which I could re-conceptualize struggle and resistance in ways that affirm and extend my ways of knowing and being. Conversations became central to my mental health, the affirmation of my mental wealth, and my vision of persistence and survivance as a Black woman-mother-scholar. This exploration is not a culmination of this reflective work, but an awakening to its resonance within my current and ancestral lived realities.

"Hey D, is the little one in the room?" I quickly turn my head to check that my six-year-old isn't peeking into the kitchen and then shake my head toward the camera on my laptop. Fortunately for the group of faces staring back at me, the little one is playing chess in the other room, far away from the expletives that sometimes pepper our conversations. I move back and forth between listening to the conversation developing in my online group, preparing dinner, and monitoring my son, who is secretly hoping that this meeting will result in the disregard of his screen time limits.

Black Women Mothering & Daughtering During a Dual Pandemic:
Writing Our Backs, pp. 41–51
Copyright © 2024 by Information Age Publishing
www.infoagepub.com
41

This scene represents my typical Sunday routine as I try to find space for (re)connecting with my voice and spirit through the drudgery and exigencies of the academic tenure track. It reflects a sensation of perpetual motion—a constant ebb and flow, interrupted periodically by the crash of waves upon my shores. I shift between obligations and expectations that define my day, trying to make space for this little one to thrive. Toute Bagai.[1]

During the last few years, I have lost my sense of self. Everything I am has become entangled in this urgency to produce, to succeed, to impress. In the farthest corners of my mind, I still wonder if I will ever be good enough to live up to the hopes and dreams of my ancestors. My life exists in overlapping pockets of time through which I flit back and forth, hoping that at the end of the day, something will be complete, something will be accomplished, and that this all has some meaning in the life I hope to lead.

As a Black woman immigrant scholar, I have always embraced the weight of the hopes of generations on my shoulders. My path represents both the culmination of the struggle and perseverance of those who paved my way and my hopes for my offspring for generations to come. I stand on the shoulders of giants, and they have given all of who they are for me to reach for my stars. Through the writing of Evans-Winters (2019), I have revisited the collective consciousness of my community (p. 37) and the conscious and unconscious performances of daughtering as a coping mechanism during times of struggle and conflict. I am the daughter of Diana, of Dorothy and Angela, of Jestina and Mabel, of Rafaela and Wilemena, and the generations of strong-backed and unflinching woman-mother-scholars that persisted through violations of the body and spirit in order for me to exist and even still, thrive. In this context, I define scholarship outside of the bounds of academia and colonization. Instead, I recognize and name their vast wisdom, informal scholarship, and extensive connections to the land, the community, and our ways of knowing and being despite centuries of displacement, enforced limitations, and disregard. Like Dillard (2014), I (re)member my grandmothers and draw from their legacy of love and strength in the face of such unwavering disfavor.

But I am tired. And the threat of failure, as I try to do too much with dwindling reserves, paralyzes me and tempts the fates. As I write this, it is not yet dawn, and I have been staring at the same page in my work sessions for over a week. I have so much to say that I fear it will emerge only as a scream of anguish, so I say nothing at all. However, as I continue my frenetic dance, trying to dodge the waves, I remember that the little one is watching. He looks at me alone in the way that I once looked upon my circle of elders, and sometimes, those glances of expectation and hope are enough to help me find balance among the tides. Like those who came before me, I choose to survive (Dillard, 2016).

As part of my expected progress in academia, I have focused on my professional responsibilities of teaching, research, and service within pockets of time while I raise my son in a space that does not embrace my whole being. However, the last year of navigating the COVID-19 pandemic has presented a shift in space and time that has allowed me to reflect and refocus my efforts around who I am and who I want to be. Somewhere along this journey, I was in the right place at the right time, and I was introduced to a group of warm and dynamic Black women in a circle of friendship, reflection, and scholarship. This circle of sisterhood has loosened my bonds and allowed the parts of me that have too long remained hidden to emerge in dendritic tendrils that accept all that I was, embrace all that I am, and guide me forward, always reminding me of the ancestors who stand behind me as a source of energy and awakening. I'm not sure what I was hoping to accomplish when I began this journey of exploration and sisterhood, but for the first time during this academic journey, I feel like I am collecting and connecting all the pieces of myself back into a full being.

Through the use of autoethnographic methods, I seek to embrace the complexities of my roles as a mother, sister, daughter, and scholar by "writ[ing] as an Other and for an Other" (Boylorn & Orbe, 2014, p. 15). I have chosen to embrace paradigms that reflect my hybridity and my reality and that "encompass and embody [my] cultural and spiritual understandings and histories and that shape [my] epistemologies and ways of being" (Dillard & Okpalaoka, 2011, p. 147). There is significance in being able to name my reality (Okpalaoka & Dillard, 2011) and embrace my cultural historicity. My culture, which is central to my reality, shapes my worldview and creates space within these paradigms for me to find and share my voice (Dillard, 2006). "How we see a thing—even with our eyes—is very much dependent on where we stand in relationship to it" (Wa Thiong'o, 1986/2008, p. 88). For me, this chapter is both a spiritual and intellectual pursuit driven by my experiences, passions, and challenges. Through my developing understanding of my African ascendency (Dillard, 2006; Dillard, 2008; Dillard, 2012; Dillard & Bell, 2011; Dillard & Okpalaoka, 2011) and its role in voicing my reality as a colonized being who still struggles within the bonds of her colonization, I harness the sacred and historic nature of endarkened and indigenous knowledges that resonates to the very core of my being. The concepts of spirituality, community, and praxis are central to endarkened and indigenous ways of knowing (Dillard, 2008; Dillard & Dixson, 2006; Tuhiwai Smith, 2012), which "can reside in bodies and cultural memories notwithstanding global migrations, globalization, and the emergence of Diasporic communities" (Sefa Dei, 2011, p. 26).

In this chapter, I reach toward the Ifa/Orisha and Kwéyòl traditions of my Trinbagonian[2] heritage to guide the reader through a series of vignettes and reflections. Each section represents, through the lens of our ancestral and extempore traditions, a blossoming of understanding as I explore my challenges and survivance (Sabzalian, 2019) navigating the academic realm during this twin pandemic of white supremacy and COVID-19 with the help of these found sisters. Sharing my voice as the daughter I am and as the mother I am becoming, I invite readers on this journey that seeks to embrace these understandings as both a tool of introspection and comfort. I am "(re)learning to name [myself] for [myself]" (Evans-Winters, 2019, p. 14). This framing represents a way of knowing, a search for completeness, and resistance to the colonial (Sefa Dei, 2011).

Santimanitay³: The Invitation

The muted strum of my alarm bleeds through to my consciousness, and I groan softly as my arm reaches beyond the warmth of layered blankets into the crisp air of the room. My eyes flutter open, and the groan increases volume as I realize that my unconscious self has already snoozed the alarm multiple times—2:45 A.M. I roll over, pulling blankets with me, and snuggle closer to the little bundle of heat and sighs that lie to my left. The familiar tune plays again, and somehow, I have lost more time—2:55 A.M. I carefully slide backward, gently removing the blankets and positioning the giant stuffed bunny who holds my space and comforts my son in my absence. I tiptoe through the darkness, pausing once to soft sounds of stirring before escaping to the dim light of the hallway. My eyes, still heavy with sleep, tense, and squint at the bright light on my laptop as I begin my workday. I only have a few hours left before he wakes, and it is time to start school.

Navigating the balance between work and remote/home school has left my body sleep-deprived and my thought patterns in disarray. It is a constant race against time as my role shifts from scholar to parent soon after sunrise. Breakfast must be made and time managed so that we can get a head-start on a day filled with college teaching, meetings, and the ever-plentiful stream of emails that fill my inbox. My body and mind scream for moments of meditation and exercise, but there are not enough hours in the day. I have to choose so my mind and body get pushed to the side as I try to survive.

I am pulled in so many directions in this life I have chosen that I am excelling in none. I worry that my writing will suffer without time to hone my skills. I worry that my son will hate me for always having something else to do and always having to schedule time to play. I worry that my students will think I am unprofessional when evidence of my real life comes into view. I worry that I am simply not enough. I feel the weight of this world, and trying to release myself feels like moving in shifting delta sands. The more I move, the more I endanger myself, so eventually, I become motionless and staring, this promise of hope seemingly unattainable.

There is never enough time. Not for scholarship, not for fun, not for life. So I make do, knowing that making do could cost me everything and bring my greatest fear—losing time to the pace—to fruition. I find myself locked firmly in the competency trap detailed by Macmillan-Cotton (2019). Every time I feel like I have reached my goal of enacting competence, the sands shift, making this delicate balance even more difficult to attain. So I stretch my being, reaching for this carrot-on-a-stick that will forever be out of reach because I will never satisfy those seeking to determine my path. Continually assessed and found deficient, there is always more to prove. My work is too humanities-centered. It is not humanities-centered enough. I do not fit within any of the neat boxes that shape the elitism of academia and cannot be included in any existing in-group because my ways of knowing and being in this world challenge the status quo and invite a level of reflection that cannot be comforted or quieted by the inconsequential chatter of polite conversation.

The claim that one has found balance in this dance of the discontented is supposed to bring comfort, but after years of reaching for this goal, I realize the fallacy of this premise. There is no balance in this space for someone like me. It is always a sense of what's next? Not because I want something else to do but because there is far too much to be done. I glance around at friends and colleagues who are spending time with loved ones and generally engaging with life outside work, and I wonder where I have gone wrong. There is a constant ebb and flow between confidence and feeling like I will never be able to be my best self because there is never enough time. All I want to do is return to a semblance of a normal life in which I sleep when it is dark and wake up rested to greet the day. I need my son to know that there is more to life than simply existing in this colonized space, but my words are hollow when I cannot even disrupt the cycle of my own undoing.

I often reflect on what would have happened and how I would have survived this pandemic without this sister circle. Even in this space of uncertainty and struggle, these women helped me claim and recognize my worthiness as they "marshal[led] the social, cultural, and spiritual strength to make ... declarations of love every day all day, to make declarations of the goodness of our existence (Dillard, 2016, p. 30). It was they who held my hand as my eyes opened to the trap in which I found myself, they who created space for rest and reflection, they who heard my silent sufferings (Dillard, 2016, p. 31), and they who helped me choose to act—to declare that I deserved more.

The Gayelle[4]: The Stage

My head jerks around to the sound of soft taps on my office door. My stomach starts to flutter a bit at the sight of my supervisor, wondering if this visit is a response to my recent email requesting an appointment. "What do you want to talk about?" I shift uncomfortably in my chair, scrunching my toes repeatedly in my shoes in an attempt to ground myself and present confidence. I take a deep breath and blurt out, "I want to talk about my workload." Silence. The quiet increases my discomfort and pushes a barrage of jumbled frustrations from my mouth as I try to highlight the unreasonable expectations set out by a constantly increasing teaching load and research expectations that remain the same. As I try to translate my frustrations with ever-changing tenure expectations into the quantified discourse he expects, I am again met with silence and this time, what might be just a hint of a nod. I rush to fill the silence, explaining the content and structure of my work and looking for any signs of acknowledgment or support. Silence. After a few seconds that seemed to stretch and swell awkwardly, I saw a firm nod. As my nerve strengthens and I straighten my back, his words leave uncertainty and confusion. "I know you can do it." I listen to the justification with restraint, pleading with my body to obscure the conflict of emotions and enveloping dread whirling inside me. As he exits, I feel my lips tremble and my confidence crash like waves at the shoreline, their power shattered against an outcrop of sharp rocks blocking a path to the sand.

There is an expectation in academia that the work can all get done if you are truly committed. Of course, that implies that being unable to rise from beneath the not-so-subtle hazing that defines the tenure track is a personal failure. It suggests that something is lacking and that I am not enough. There is the constant sense of assuming that I can take just one more task, help one more student, carry one more weight, and hold on through yet another rip tide that seeks to yank me away from the relative safety of the ever-shifting sand. There is nothing, absolutely nothing, that keeps me safe in this space.

Macmillan Cottom's (2019) discussion of how the competency trap lures many of us who just want to be seen and valued revisits the racist and sexist perception of Black women as strong and invulnerable. While reading her work with my group of found sisters, I wondered how much of the perception that I could handle my workload without intervention was based on a lack of understanding about the complexities of my lived realities and how much was centered on the notion that my back was broad enough to carry the load. In this context, I take on the role of the famed superhero; I am "successful but not happy" (p. 93), accomplished but not fulfilled, wise yet infantile.

The quantity of my publications is constantly compared to those who do not share my entanglements: parents of grown children, colleagues without children, and the ever-present married male who can write for days in a row because of the support of a significant other who shoulders the burdens of domestic life. My child, this small human that helps the world make sense, is seen as an obstacle that I have to overcome. If I would just focus on the work, they say there is enough time. This sense that time is only valuable when outcomes can be immediately quantified is discordant with my ways of mothering and daughtering and pushes me away from traditions that ground my cultural self (Evans-Winters, 2019). If this child is a burden, then he is my burden to carry, and I will carry him high on my shoulders so that one day he can fly.

These always-increasing expectations feel like sabotage. For every success I have, I am punished within a system that devalues my ways of knowing and being. To complete the high-quality work I want to pursue, I need to critically reflect on the ways in which my being connects or disengages with the world and works of others while simultaneously loving and guiding this shining life. But that time always feels just outside my reach.

Within the collective of my chosen Sisters, however, I found solace and understanding. Was this because of our shared sense of becoming, or had I finally found space in which I could find the breath to speak my truth? Whatever the reason the ancestors have for bringing me into this space, it has steeled my resolve and recentered the path of my womanhood and my scholarship. I will not let this place and its policies break me. Those who came before me survived greater challenges than mine, and the power of their blood runs in my veins. I can and will name my oppressions and confront them with this army at my back.

The Lavway[5]: Preparing for Battle

"Laventille Road, Laventille Road in de mornin'.… Is 5 o'clock in de mornin', 5 o'clock in de mornin.'" As the chant continues on the screen where the pandemic has blessed us with cultural engagement via Zoom, I watch my son instinctively rise and start to dance to the rhythms of the drums played by the young men of Kambule Campus.[6] His tiny feet try to keep up with the quickening tempo, and tears well up in my eyes as his hands extend above his head, waving back and forth. I rise too and start to dance. I close my eyes and listen to the language of the drums. They speak of pain and terror, of love and loss, of redemption and triumph. They tell the story of those who came across the seas and of those who leaped to their deaths on that journey rather than face a lifetime of bondage. They tell the story of my grandmother, a practitioner of the Ifa/Orisha tradition, who, like many, adopted Catholicism after the practice of our ancestral religions and celebrations was labeled a crime. They tell the story of (re)birth and (re)visioning, and all at once, as my head falls backward, I feel release. I feel the embrace of all who have come before me, and I see their blood in my son's veins. This (re)membering, is about "an awakening, an opening to the spirit of something that has, until that moment, been asleep within us" (Dillard, 2012, p. 3)

In that moment, I embraced my (re)membering and (re)visioning, call-ing on the ancestors to guide my path and bless the journey of the little one. I find myself now, like Dillard, reflecting and questioning, "Who Am I?" Who Are We?" This group of sisters has brought back memories that have been suppressed as I navigate the world of the Other and as an Other. This chosen Sister circle has created something for which my very soul yearned: space and time. This connective and collective memory-making has helped me name my ancestral identities and has fostered the transformation that I can sense coming.

As I move with the call of the bembe,[7] my role in this space of mother-daughter-learner, has never been clearer. As I let my body relive rhythms and sensations not felt for many years, I feel the chains lift off my soul and for a moment, I am completely free. I feel the winds surge through me, bringing the ancestors directly to this space, and I smile. As the drums cease their rhythms, the little one continues to sing the refrain, and I tilt my head at the realization that this U.S.-born child has never set foot on Laventille Road and probably never will. The town of Laventille, once one of the most prosperous towns in the West Indies, inhabited primarily by formerly enslaved Africans post-Emancipation, has fallen into disrepute and heavy crime due to decades of societal and systemic marginalization. Although a few members of my family still reside there in the birthplace of the steelpan, I was discouraged from visiting during my last trip for my safety. I mourn this loss for my son while celebrating the strength of resistance that runs in our veins. We are fighters. We are reclaimers who play the long game. We will survive.

Las' Lap[8]: The Wrap-Up

As my semester got underway, midway through writing this chapter, the responsibilities and weight of the academic tenure track seemed simultaneously more tangible yet more manageable than before. I approached the semester with renewed vigor, and while the tides may move me as they wish, I am supported by the buoyancy shared in the space created by this reading and discussion group. I have taken some valuable lessons with me as I walk toward my futures, and I have learned to take moments to put myself and my family first.

My academic load has not changed. The racism and elitism I manage at work and in my community has not changed. The strain of homeschooling my son while doing this all alone has not changed. But I have. Inspired by the readings we have done as a group, I have re-embraced my love of myself and the ideas and ideals that I bring to the spaces I inhabit. Whereas before I focused on the difficult journey ahead, the experience of navigating these pandemics with this sister circle reminded me of the boost from below that my histories provide—the support that I forgot, for a while, was forever at my side. I am starting to (re)claim my space in small ways through simple but neglected hobbies like reading, not just because it enriches my teaching or research, but because it brings me joy.

I have not met with the sister circle in over two months, and I have noticed their absence. Those two hours on a Sunday that I carved despite my packed schedule were more critical than I could ever have imagined, and without them, though my strength stays true, the pangs of loneliness have returned—ever stronger now that I have had a taste of possibility. I have faced more conflict since we last met, but when unsure, it is their faces that I see and their voices that push me forward on the winds of the ancestors. There is a revelation here about not only the source of our strengths but also about the catalysts that allow us to rise when the weight of our burdens feels inescapable. One thing I know for sure: Thanks to the space created by these sisters, I am (re)membering myself and forging a new path through the barriers before me.

Throughout this journey, embracing Evans-Winters's (2019) conceptualization of daughtering as a coping mechanism during times of struggle and conflict has guided me through two of the toughest years of my adult life. Daughtering, as a spiritual and cultural process contextualized by my experiential knowledge, allows me to invoke the power of all that I am, all that we were, and all that we will be. Through the readings and conversations with these sister scholars, I am creating space to balance the needs of my chosen profession and my institution with my personal and communal struggle for liberation. Toute Bagai.

REFERENCES

Boylorn, R. M., & Orbe. M. P. (2014). Critical autoethnography as method of choice. In R. M Boylorn & M. P. Orbe (Eds.), *Critical autoethnography: Intersecting cultural identities in everyday life* (pp. 13–26). Left Coast Press.

Dillard, C. B. (2006). When the music changes, so should the dance: Cultural and spiritual considerations in paradigm 'proliferation'. *International Journal of Qualitative Studies in Education, 19*(1), 59–76.

Dillard, C. B. (2008). When the ground is black, the ground is fertile: Exploring endarkened feminist epistemology and healing methodologies of the spirit. In N. K. Denzin, Y. S. Lincoln, & L. Tuhiwai Smith (Eds.), *Handbook of critical and indigenous methodologies* (pp. 277–292). SAGE.

Dillard, C. B. (2012). *Learning to (re)member the things we've learned to forget: Endarkened feminisms, spirituality, & the sacred nature of research & teaching*. Peter Lang.

Dillard, C. B. (2014). (Re)membering the grandmothers: Theorizing poetry to (re)think the purposes of black education and research. In N. K. Denzin & M. D. Giardina (Eds.), *Qualitative inquiry outside the academy* (pp. 253–267). Routledge.

Dillard, C. B. (2016). To address suffering that the majority can't see: Lessons from black women's leadership in the workplace. *New Directions for Adult And Continuing Education, 152,* 29–38.

Dillard, C. B., & Bell, C. (2011). Endarkened feminism and sacred practice: Troubling (auto) ethnography through critical engagements with African indigenous knowledges. In G. J. Sefa Dei (Ed.), *Indigenous philosophies and critical education* (pp. 337–349). Peter Lang.

Dillard, C. B., & Dixson, A. D. (2006). Affirming the will and the way of the ancestors. Black feminist consciousness and the search for "good"[ness] in qualitative science. In N. K. Denzin & M. D. Giardina (Eds.), *Qualitative inquiry and the conservative challenge* (pp. 227–254). Left Coast Press.

Dillard, C. B., & Okpalaoka, C. L. (2011). The sacred and spiritual nature of Endarkened transnational feminist praxis in qualitative research. In N. K. Denzin & Y. S. Lincoln (Eds.), *The Sage handbook of qualitative research* (4th ed., pp. 147–162). SAGE.

Evans-Winters, V. E. (2019). *Black feminism in qualitative inquiry: A mosaic for writing our daughter's body.* Routledge.

Macmillan Cottom, T. (2019). *Thick.* The New Press.

Okpalaoka, C. L., & Dillard, C. B. (2011). Our healing is next to the wound: Endarkened feminisms, spirituality, and wisdom for teaching, learning, and research. *New Directions for Adult and Continuing Education, 131,* 65–74.

Sabzalian, L. (2019). *Indigenous children's survivance in public schools.* Taylor & Francis.

Sefa Dei, G. J. (2011). Revisiting the question of the 'indigenous'. In G. J. Sefa Dei (Ed.), *Indigenous philosophies and critical education* (pp. 21–33). Peter Lang.

Tuhiwai Smith, L. (2012). *Decolonizing methodologies: Research and indigenous peoples* (2nd ed.). Zed Books.

Wa Thiong'o, N. (2008). *Decolonising the mind: The politics of language in African literature.* James Currey. (Original work published 1986)

ENDNOTES

1. Toute Bagai is a French patois expression in Trinidad & Tobago meaning everything (as in: Everything but the kitchen sink).
2. Trinbagonian and a people from the twin-island republic of Trinidad & Tobago
3. Santimanita ia a traditional Kalinda and Calypso challenge refrain from Trinidad & Tobago (French sans humanité "without mercy"). Extempo calypsonians, who improvise lyrics on the spot, would end their stanzas with this refrain to indicate its end and also as an invitation to their competitor to engage with the song.
4. Gayell in the Kalinda tradition of Trinidad and Tobago (stick-fighting). This is a safe space to find identity through conflict.
5. The Trinidad definition of Lavway is a collection of songs, a selection of battle hymns. Lavway is the people voicing their spirituality; they are guided by the singer or Chantuelle.

6. Kambule Campus was an online workshop series in late 2020/early 2021 from the Idakeda Group, Ltd. that creates and hosts multidisciplinary cultural events. This series focused on the ritual and performance arts of Trinidad Carnival, grounded in African traditions.
7. Bembe is the lead drum.
8. Las' Lap is the final round of celebration during the Trinidad Carnival that represents the last hour of the traditional festivities prior to the start of Lent.

CHAPTER 5

THERAPY SESSIONS

Observations and Reflections of a Black Psychotherapist's Experience During COVID-19

Angela R. Clack

In this chapter, I share reflections as a Black psychotherapist supporting clients and therapists during the COVID-19 pandemic. I am guided by my practice to hold space for clients and clinicians both white and Black who are simultaneously working through their experiences of grief, loss, and trauma. The intersection of three pandemics: (1) a Black mental health crisis; (2) White supremacy, police brutality, political unrest; and (3) a global public health crisis—led to Black therapist burnout. The demands and needs for therapy and mental health in marginalized communities outweighed the number of Black therapists who could help. My participation in a Black women's literature circle helped me cope with the traumatic stress of multiple crises. I learned to re-conceptualize Black women's mental health through the lens of de-constructing systems that historically have oppressed our intellect, abused our bodies, and imprisoned our minds.

"Is solace anywhere more comforting than that in the arms of my sister?"

—Alice Walker

Black Women Mothering & Daughtering During a Dual Pandemic: Writing Our Backs, pp. 53–61
Copyright © 2024 by Information Age Publishing
www.infoagepub.com
All rights of reproduction in any form reserved.

I am a healer and trauma-informed clinician who has been in the mental health field for over three decades. I embrace the embodied work of being a somatic healer that integrates mind, body, soul, and spiritual practices. I recognize that colonized approaches are harmful and dismissive as they minimize and pathologize our African cultural roots, histories, spiritualities, and experiences. Now more than ever, we face a significant mental health crisis at the height of anti-Blackness when we need it most.

In her book, *The Unapologetic Guide to Black Mental Health*, Dr. Rheeda Walker (2020) writes, "Instead of paying attention to your feelings of anxiety or depression, or the signs of distress, you press forward. You remind yourself that Black people persevere" (p. 10). Dr. Walker asserted that even within a society of racial terrorism, "you continue on using your ancestral gifts" (p. 10). Hearing her words made me reflect on Paul Laurence Dunbar's poetry. Dunbar's poem, "We Wear the Mask" reflects the generations that endured pain but hid it behind smiles. I assert that strength, also known as *Superwoman Syndrome,* has become synonymous with struggle for Black women. Black women walk through life wounded, wearing the denial and suppression of pain like a badge of honor.

Therapy Sessions is my narrative as a Black therapist treating clinicians and clients of color through racial trauma, medical and mental health disparities, anxiety, and uncertainty amid a global pandemic. This is the same America that has been and continues to assault Black and Brown bodies with little accountability or regard for human rights. Amid a virus killing thousands of Black Americans, we were faced with a betrayal of the U.S. Constitution that claims "justice for all" but murdered Blacks innocent people like Breonna Taylor and George Floyd. To help myself during this time, I sought safety, support, and validation in a literature circle with other Black women.

I am typically the "nice Black woman" in the room. I will not deny that being a lighter-complexioned woman creates a different stimulus for white people. I am no stranger to the benefits and attacks of colorism in our world. I am that one who finds confrontation difficult at times. However, during the pandemic, there was increasing dismissiveness and lack of regard for Black women, and finding my voice has taken on a new charge. I found myself advocating more and more and helping Black women in therapy to "be stronger advocates" for themselves against racial insults and assaults, micro and microaggressions, and invalidations. The work became more exhausting as more and more Black people needed support. Black women were experiencing anxiety and depression more profoundly and were more in need than two years prior. I found myself seeing more and more clients and taking on more and more work. I felt obligated. I felt the burden and joy of "rescuing" my community from white people and therapists who could not relate. Not soon enough, I found myself not well physically and emotionally. My mind and body were drained. The Black Women's Mental Wealth Academy helped me in this challenging and sensitive climate.

In the Black Women's Mental Wealth Academy—a collective sisterhood healing circle of intelligent, beautiful professional Black women storytellers and authors—we used our reading circle to give voice to our narratives in this timely and well-researched anthology. My sister writers are academicians (educators and college professors) and literary artists in a sister circle group I joined at the start of the COVID-19 pandemic.

I have come at the subject matter through a unique lens in this anthology. I offer the reader the clinical insights and observations of a Black, Indigenous Person of Color (BIPOC) and psychotherapist treating Black and Brown bodies and white people while living and working through the same conditions of COVID-19. I accepted with gratitude the invitation to join this sisterhood in writing at an unprecedented historical period at the intersection of a pandemic (COVID-19), the Black mental health crisis, and the persistent and pervasive racist assaults against Black and Brown bodies. I also offer my lived experience of living in Black skin as a woman during the emotional impact of the pandemic.

When I wrote my first self-published narrative in 2018 (Clack, 2018) on the reconceptualization of Black women and trauma and depression, I intended to ignite a conversation, a movement away from the colonizers' language and definitions of Black mental health and toward radical, culturally responsive, and sensitive healing. Healing would promote restructuring a system that ignores and dismisses the transmission of intergenerational trauma and depression. Healing would lead to requiring white professionals who serve People of Color do the necessary work to understand them emotionally, spiritually, and intrapsychically before labeling, medicating, and over-diagnosing. Medicine has a long history of bias and mistreatment of people of color. Dr. Joy DeGruy spent 12 years researching the residual impact of generations of slavery and developed her theory of *post-traumatic slave syndrome*. She published her findings in her critically acclaimed book, *Post Traumatic Slave Syndrome-America's Legacy of Injury and Healing* (2017). Dr. DeGruy's theory explains the etiology of the adaptive survival behaviors of African American communities throughout the U.S. and the Diaspora. She describes it as a condition resulting from the multigenerational oppression of Africans and their descendants from centuries of chattel slavery. She goes on to say that slavery produced centuries of physical, psychological, and spiritual injury. She speaks to the multigenerational patterns of adaptive behaviors passed through generations and the need for clinicians and other service providers to engage in assessments and interventions using evidence-based, culturally specific, and social justice models and frameworks.

Dr. Walker also stated that we thrive despite harsh and inhumane treatment. We tap into something cultivated for generations. When our ancestors struggled to live to the next day, endure mistreatment, and be themselves without consequences, there was no time for emotional problems. The suppression of pain began in slavery. Is it no wonder Black people have tremendous mistrust towards white medical institutions, doctors, and therapists? History has shown us that we cannot trust healthcare providers who do not look like us and negate, deny, dismiss, destroy, and distort our stories.

In March 2020, our lives changed instantly and dramatically. One month prior, I was enjoying the beautiful island of Kauai, Hawaii, as a workshop presenter. I was not mentally prepared for what happened less than three weeks after my return. Within weeks, the whole country was shut down. Our roles as therapists, helpers, and healers left us scrambling to make immediate adjustments to how mental health and medical professionals had traditionally conducted business. Therapists began to counsel and support individuals and families through a global pandemic (COVID-19) and an economic crisis reminiscent of a second Great Depression. Additionally, a politically polarized election created division along party lines among family members, friends, and co-workers. With no time to prepare mentally or physically, we all simultaneously attempted to adjust to our personal experiences of the same crises amid a racial (in)justice movement, significant mental health, and public health crisis. These events culminated in a global collective trauma response of chronic uncertainty, anxiety, depression, grief, and trauma.

Enter spring 2020. Here are some of the topics and headlines that were being discussed by global news media outlets such as CNBC, Centers for Disease Control & Prevention, Center for Infectious Disease Research and Policy, and Penn Today:

- Researchers are warning that the coronavirus pandemic could inflict long-lasting emotional trauma on an unprecedented global scale.
- The COVID-19 crisis has combined mental health stressors that have been studied before in other disasters but have never been consolidated in one global crisis, experts in trauma psychology said.
- "The scale of this outbreak as a traumatic event is almost beyond comprehension," said one expert.
- Black Americans are getting sick and dying from COVID-19 at higher rates than white Americans—the most recent manifestation of racial health disparities that have long been evident in

the United States. U.S. blacks are three times more likely than whites to get COVID-19.

- COVID-19's assault on Black and Brown communities: Racism, inequality, and the coronavirus have combined to cause an alarming number of COVID-19 cases and deaths among African American and Latinx populations.

*On January 6, 2020, right in the middle of writing this chapter, another chaotic disruption of racism, violence, and display of white supremacy and white privilege erupted in our nation's Capital. Headline: **A pro-Trump mob stormed the Capitol. After fleeing for their safety, members of Congress voted to confirm Biden's victory.** They (rioters) fought their way through armed police, smashed windows, and stormed the U.S. Capitol to prevent Congress from certifying President-elect Joe Biden's victory. They (Trump supporters and rioters) spent several hours inside the building, vandalizing offices, and the House floor. Trump, speaking (insert: inciting and encouraging) to the protestors at a rally hours before they burst into the Capitol, referred to his political opponents as "bad people" and "the enemy of the people." He described his allies as "warriors" and encouraged them to stop "fighting like a boxer with his hands tied behind his back." He added, "We're going to have to fight much harder."*

This occurred in real-time, and what we witnessed continues to unsettle and traumatize our very existence as Black people in White America under the siege of white supremacy.

What you will read below are thoughts and words directly quoted and expressed by Black therapists in response to a social media post asking about their coping and self-care during the pandemic.

- *Exhausted.*
- *Angry.*
- *Tired of white privilege and white supremacy.*
- *Processing events with clients was very emotional.*
- *Disbelief. I feel sick.*
- *I'm numb and detached.*
- *My patients are triggered.*
- *BLM (Black Lives Matter) protestors are gassed, beaten, and killed, but you can commit treason ... sedition, and if you're white, it's ok.*
- *Is it unethical to screen out clients for having racist ideologies.*

The social media posts continued with ongoing expressions of therapists' pain and frustration. Social media during this time became one of the largest platforms for support due to social distancing and physical restrictions mandates. In one Facebook community for Black clinicians,

Clinicians of Color in Private Practice, a Black therapist comment summed it up so well:

> My afternoon session hit really different after the breaking news at the Capitol. As a Black woman therapist, sitting with, holding, and providing space for other Black women is an honor, but it is a burden that is so hard to carry when the world is on fire. Today we just sat together in the heaviness. The amount of pivoting we have to do to show up is challenging. I count it both a blessing and a burden. But if not us … who else?

Today, Black people continue to struggle and find significant challenges in seeking safety and support for emotional and physical healing from trauma. Even the Black church, which has traditionally been a prominent place for protection and healing, previously our ancestors' route to safe passage to freedom, is the target of racist attacks and domestic terrorism. Being kidnapped from our native land, tortured, abused, raped, branded, and mutilated, we were robbed of everything that once was our saving grace, our ethnic identity, and freedom. Our history has left us with painful experiences and legacies that we have passed down to generations through epigenetics, modeling, and storytelling. The mental and medical health systems have historically failed people of color by adopting racist and discriminatory policies, procedures, and practices that significantly impact the type and quality of care these communities receive. These environments where treatment is provided are often covered by mental health practitioners and medical providers that, through explicit or implicit bias, perpetuate discriminatory practices that lead to the misdiagnosis, mistreatment, and under-treatment of the presenting problem.

During the pandemic, particularly at the height of racial injustice and unrest, in reading many social media posts and emotionally charged comments and thoughts shared publicly in protest. As an act of resistance, I have also found this particularly challenging in our field. I, too, find it a blessing and a burden to hold space for a Black client whose suffering is compounded by the inequities and disparities in access to health care, the persistent and pervasive racist assaults, microaggressions, and the stark reality that there are not enough Black therapists to meet the overwhelming demands of Black people seeking help. The burden to the Black therapist, who out of their commitment to the community, is trying to help everyone, leaving the therapist emotionally and physically exhausted. Burned out.

Dr. Joy Harden Bradford is a Black licensed clinical psychologist, speaker, and the founder of the Therapy for Black Girls online mental health platform, community, and podcast. Her work makes mental health topics more relevant and accessible for Black women and girls. She started with a blog by the same name in 2014 that evolved into a movement and campaign to support Black women's mental wellness. I learned about her work through her therapist directory, which lists nationwide mental health providers specializing in working with black women and girls. As an additional resource, Dr. Joy created an online membership community, Sister Circle, that creates a sense of belonging and connection through sisterhood that focuses on mental well-being. This is the first large-scale resource connecting Black women with therapists who look like them.

Even with so many therapists and women connecting through her community and platform, the mental health needs of Black women were overwhelming, as the demands for help far exceeded available resources during the pandemic. For the first time, many Black women who had been struggling with depression and anxiety throughout the pandemics decided to seek help. Unfortunately, many licensed mental health providers like me are overwhelmed with meeting our communities' emotional and mental needs. We have long waitlists because Black women prefer to meet with Black therapists. It would help if there were more therapists of color, yet only about 4% of all practicing psychologists in America are African American (Lin et al., 2018). Increasing the number of clinicians of color will be critical to improving treatment outcomes and public health disparities for Black communities. Furthermore, additional research is needed to assess the prevalence of mental illness in women of color and the gender disparities that exist within the same-race cohorts. Little has been written about race and ethnicity in the therapeutic relationship. It has been suggested that less attention has been paid to this issue because patients and clinicians of color are underrepresented.

I end this narrative as I started. It remains clear that many Black clients/patients prefer Black therapists to treat their mental health concerns. More clinicians of color groups and resources with clinicians of color directories are being created through online and social media platforms and a web presence. Therapists of color remain in high demand as the needs of communities of color increase exponentially due to community and interpersonal violence, racial trauma, social injustices, and health disparities, particularly those with poor access to mental and physical healthcare. There is not much research on how available white therapists are for the Black client who needs to process racial trauma, nor for Black therapists in managing their feelings in working with racist white clients. What is important is how we, as healers, practice not just self-care, but radical self-care as an act of resistance. Alternatives to mental health therapy will need to be supported and considered. Healing circles, like the Black Women's Mental Wealth Academy, held space for me and my emotions when I did not have therapy. This does not replace the professional and therapeutic relationship between the therapist (licensed mental health professional) and the client. However, it is an adjunct to a type of support system that is powerful in healing.

Many of our guided exercises were powerful in helping me to reclaim who I am in my identity as a Black woman and my worth and value as a therapist of color. In one exercise, we were assigned to read Alice Walker's (1990), *The Temple of My Familiar*. We were charged to reflect on what she taught us about Western culture and representations of reality. The group was led to look for ways we saw ourselves in the story. This exercise explored what resonated with us and expanded into exploring the psychology of color. One of the more powerful exercises allowed us to be playful and creative. With the amount of traumatic stress we were under, this was precisely what was needed. Creativity and play are powerful coping tools and communal healing practices to integrate whole-body engagement on both sides of the brain. We were instructed to use a metaphor to describe how we felt as of that day (August 30, 2020). I drew a beautiful vase with flowers and butterflies on the outside. I wrote the following: This beautiful container "holds" so much of others' stuff, others' stories, and others' pain while trying to make space and room for my story, my peace, my wellness, and my identity. On the outside, it is well-constructed and beautiful, but on the inside, it is worn. No one can see inside it, and no one is even curious about the inside because they would be deceived." There it is! The ugly imposter syndrome that torments Black women in their souls. The reading circle assignment and the discussions allowed me to uncover some truths I had never spoken to anyone. The emotional safety curated by the group provided many opportunities for parts of myself to be vulnerable. It opened to deeper connections within me and between the sisters in the reading circle. The common theme was seeing myself as a "container." I continue to use this metaphor as a framework for living life authentically. This is revolutionary for a Black woman first to cultivate the belief in herself. I am learning to check in with my sense of self first.

With my gratitude, I thank my griot sisters for the invitation to speak to and narrate what my life has looked like for more than a year. As a therapist of color, it has been heavy, and many days I have felt overwhelmed and burdened by being unable to be more present for the overwhelming need. Nevertheless, as I recite the old gospel lyrics by Reverend Clay Evans, "As I look back over my life, and I think things over, I can truly say that I've been blessed … I've got a testimony."

REFERENCES

Clack, A. (2018). *Women of color talk: Psychological narratives on trauma and depression.* Clack Associates.

DeGruy, J. (2017). *Post-traumatic slave syndrome: America's legacy of injury and healing.* Joy DeGruy.

Lin, L., Stamm, K., & Christidis, P. (2018, February 1). How diverse is the psychology workforce? *Monitor on Psychology, 49*(2). https://www.apa.org/monitor/2018/02/datapoint

Walker, A. (1990). *The temple of my familiar.* Mariner Books.

Walker, R. (2020). *The unapologetic guide to Black mental health: Navigate an unequal system, learn tools for emotional wellness, and get the help you deserve.* New Harbinger Publications.

CHAPTER 6

POSSESSING A HIGHER CONSCIOUSNESS

Restoring the Spiritual Center in Civic Praxis

Sabrina J. Curtis

This chapter is an autobiographical account of my experiences as a Black woman navigating the dissertation process in the midst of dual racial and global health pandemics. I draw on *daughtering* (Evans-Winters, 2019)—a theoretical framework, marker of identity, and methodological process for recognizing how *the spiritual* affects the interconnected nature of the physical, behavioral, material, and intellectual aspects of our lives—to explore how I am positioned as a Black woman working at the intersections of Black feminist theory and critical civic praxis. In this discussion, I interrogate the social, cultural, and spiritual tensions along my journey to becoming a community engaged scholar. I further reflect on my literary engagements with sister scholars in a Black woman's book circle and how our community became a space of elevation and healing, which reignited my sense of purpose and belonging.

The spring of 2020 marked the start of a new decade ripe with birth, sickness, death, and, to some extent, renewal. The onset of a global pandemic brought us back inside just as many of us sought to emerge from the cover of winter. Our sense of being and living was collectively restructured, and our rapidly changing lives altered the way we see, view, and

Black Women Mothering & Daughtering During a Dual Pandemic:
Writing Our Backs, pp. 63–74
Copyright © 2024 by Information Age Publishing
www.infoagepub.com

navigate our world. For many, lives were torn apart by the loss of friends, family members, and mothers. The loss of jobs, peace, and security, left us with gaping holes in our lives once filled with love, sense of purpose, and desire. Spring was supposed to be the end of a season for me—one in which I sacrificed so much time, emotional strength, and physical energy to pursue a doctoral degree in an attempt to bring new life and direction to my academic career. Instead, I found myself contemplating whether the experience had been worth it and wondering where I would end up next.

This was the year I would defend my dissertation, hoping to join the company of many Black women before me who dared to enter academia in pursuit of deeper knowledge and in service to the many students like me who desired to know, do, and serve a bit more. This was my season of change. It turned out, however, to be a year of unexpected and frequently unwelcome loss and grief, compounded by uncertainty and detachment. The onset of the COVID-19 pandemic and its rapid spread across our communities changed us and the way we live. It complicated how we engage in communal practices, which allowed for closeness, commiseration, consolation, and even celebration. The material and spiritual aspects of being in community took on new meanings, and for many of us who need to *feel* others to be alive, we had to grapple with the strangeness of being alone. As a result of the conditions in which it would become too harmful to ourselves and others to be in close proximity with one another, many businesses, restaurants, universities, and schools closed in efforts to slow the spread of a highly contagious virus, which at the time, in our nation alone, claimed over a half of million lives, and counting. The sudden closure of college campuses across the country, including my own, made me realize how much of my life and memories I had already been missing.

At the time, I was completing my dissertation while balancing online teaching assistant responsibilities and serving on various committees in my graduate school as a student representative while relocating to a different state, a disruption I was unprepared for. Despite there being little change to my workload, I found myself working more slowly and reflecting much more. I was distracted by the heaviness of a time in which so many lives were lost to what seemed to be unmanageable plagues ripping through our communities. My academic commitments began to weigh on me, but not in ways fear for my family did as the COVID-19 pandemic raged on.

During this time, emotions I attempted to suppress about missing life moments and opportunities to just *be* or to be with my family in the previous three years since I began my doctoral journey began to resurface. I recounted the professional opportunities I declined as a result of starting my studies and mourned the loss of the professional and personal identity I once had. Soon, I would have to make critical decisions about what I would do next and where I would go once I graduated, but some days, it all seemed inconsequential, given the state of the world. In the following discussion, I reflect on how my literary engagements with the texts encountered in a Black women's book circle helped me to make sense of contradictions that overwhelmed my sense of self and purpose in pursuing my academic research. In framing this discussion in relation to theoretical tenets of *daughtering* and *Black feminist theory*, I interrogate the social, cultural, and spiritual tensions in my journey of becoming a community-engaged scholar and discuss how connecting with Black women scholars guided me towards resituating my work at the intersections of the political and spiritual undertakings of Black women's community work.

Theoretical Engagements

"Kinship requires responsibility" (Evans-Winters, 2019, p. 138). In *Black Feminism in Qualitative Inquiry*, Dr. Venus Evans-Winters (2019) espouses a theoretical and methodological framework that articulates how *daughtering* as both identity and process is a paradigm for recognizing how *the spiritual* affects the interconnected nature of the physical, behavioral, material, and intellectual aspects of our lives. Deriving from the interpersonal, inter-generational, and interconnected nature of Africana people's community structures and value sets, daughtering, as identity and process, requires ethical commitments to familial and community engagement, personal and professional pursuits, and to inquiry, research, analysis, and reporting (Evans-Winters, 2019).

As a Black woman whose epistemological standpoints are deeply influenced by my personal experiences and spiritual effects, I read daughtering as a form of Black feminist praxis. The Black feminist theoretical underpinnings of daughtering and Black feminist praxis center on the lived experiences of Black women, the analysis and critique of social, cultural, and political institutions, and how Black women are situated within multiple and simultaneously operating systems of oppression in which their racial and gender identities inherently compromise their physical, intellectual, social, and economic security (Collins, 1996; Collins, 2000; Evans-Winters, 2019; Guy-Sheftall, 1995; hooks, 1991).

Black feminist praxis is concerned with the theoretical implications of Black women's lives, including their spiritual endeavors and commitments to liberation (Collins, 2000; Dillard, 2000; Evans-Winters & Esposito, 2010; hooks, 1990, 2003; Walker, 1983). Dillard's (2000, 2018) theorizing of the material conditions of Black women's lives and spiritual pursuits, which she articulates through her construction of an endarkened feminist epistemology, provides a framework for examining Black women's intellectual work and spiritual reawakening. Dillard (2000) reframes research as a cultural endeavor and as "an ideological undertaking, one deeply embedded within the traditions, perspectives, viewpoints, and cultural understandings, and discourse style of the researcher" (pp. 662–663). Similarly, daughtering is a process through which we come to know who we are and how we are in the world through the observation of social practices and cultural norms, and through the uptake of community and cultural knowledge, values, spiritual practices, shared navigational skills, and particular nuances of familial data passed down by mothers, daughters, aunts, grandmothers, and othermothers.

Relying on daughtering and Black feminist theory as theoretical foundations for this discussion, I explore how my spirituality, and by extension my childhood engagement in a religious family, is central to my understanding of how I position myself as a researcher and how I come to engage in research with Black girls in community. In my attempt to reread a small aspect of my work in my dissertation research, I articulate how my engagement with literature in a Black women's book circle helped me remember and relearn how to center my cultural and spiritual self in my intellectual pursuits.

Black Feminist Praxis for the Future

One Sunday afternoon, I gathered online with a collective of women who, by the grace of God, I imagine (and mostly through the pull, coordination, light, and divine insight of Dr. Evans-Winters), helped us find one another. At the beginning of 2020, Dr. V convened a group of sister scholars in an online space that began as a book circle and evolved into a nurturing space for intellectual thought, teaching, and learning, and further into a sacred space of healing, pride, love, and joy. This space functioned as a literacy collaborative (Muhammad & Haddix, 2016), allowing for the cultivation of literacy, identity, and social development. Historically, Black women formed literacy groups that functioned as a place for reading and critique of literature but also as a space for "self-affirmation, growth, and healing" (Muhammad & Haddix, 2016, p. 312).

Black feminist theorizing emerged from the analysis of Black women's everyday activities, resistance, and advocacy (Collins, 2000). Black feminist theories and ideologies pertaining to our race and gender consciousness were also found in Black women's self-help, literacy, cultural, political, and abolitionist societies, which were formed in response to their denied membership to Black men's and white women's organizations (Guy-Sheftall, 1995).

Literacy groups, much like the ones identified above, are spaces of possibility that offer Black women the opportunity to engage in the reading and production of creative texts (in their infinite forms) and to participate in the construction of discourses that disrupt mainstream Eurocentric ideologies that obscure the literacies, creative potential, and political agency of Black women. What emerged from our book circle's initial convenings was a manifestation of Evans-Winters's (personal communication, July 2, 2020) idea of *Black women's mental wealth*. Black women's mental wealth is an intellectual and physical space, methodological approach, and conceptual framework for illuminating Black women's (at their discretion) critical and political literacies, spiritual practices, and feminist or womanist theorizing in ways that speak back to hegemonic discourses that are misrepresentative of our personal, professional, material, and spiritual pursuits.

As a collective, some of the texts guiding our discussions included Toni Morrison's (2019) collection of essays, *The Source of Self-Regard*, which followed our reading of Alice Walker's *Temple of My Familiar* and Venus Evans-Winters's (2019) *Black Feminism in Qualitative Inquiry*, texts that prompted deep reflection on sisterhood, mother-daughter relationships, and Black women's politics. In discussing the relevance of these ideas to our everyday roles and responsibilities as daughters, mothers, teachers, artists, and creatives, we contemplated the question: What does it mean to possess a higher consciousness?

At the time, I could not recall if there had been any prior occasions where I openly reflected on my identity, my Blackness, my childhood, the complexity of mother-daughter connections, and the phenomenon of being and existing as Black women in the academy with women whom I had not known previously. By virtue of our commitments and desires to show up authentically in this space, we shared many hours with one another, deeply engaging with what it means to move beyond our material realities and contemplate the spiritual, intellectual, and emotional significance of who we are and the work that we do. I found in this space that Morrison's (2019) writing gave me language to process the intellectual and interpersonal violence I had encountered at several junctures on the road to completing my dissertation, but her work also led me back to a point of understanding that while the weight of my personal experiences loomed large at times, collectively working with Black women to interrogate and disrupt the exclusionary and oppressive practices found in higher education meant that together we could chart out a pathway forward.

Literary Encounters

The stories we shared with one another in our book circle were inspired by our reading of texts written by a cadre of Black women whose intellectual pursuits resulted in the development of theoretical and conceptual frameworks centering the lived experiences, politicization, social engagement, and cultural commitments of Black people, and Black women, in particular. In the essay "The Foreigner's Home," Morrison (2019) calls our attention to how Black writers have always grappled with questions of race and gender, the dilemma of the outsider within, and the paradox of feeling "'foreign" at home. These questions continue to surface in my work in community with Black girls, especially as I try to make sense of this question of belonging in a society that continues to sideline our social, civic, and political efforts and marginalize the voices of Black women and girls. In the following sections, I share how my reflections on Morrison's (2019) essays transformed the setting into a space of elevation and healing for me that reignited my sense of purpose and belonging. I recall how finding community with other Black women sister scholars during dual racial and global health pandemics helped me remember what I had lost in my journey to completing my doctoral studies.

A Mother's Legacy and Ancestral Gifts

I enter the discourse on daughtering and Black feminist praxis as an educator, a student of literature, a community-engaged scholar, and a daughter whose mother nurtured her literary curiosities and social justice commitments from a very young age. In *Black Feminism in Qualitative Inquiry*, Evans-Winters (2019) contends that a Black feminist social justice ideology calls for "individuals who have a fighting spirit; those who are able to identify, name, and creatively confront racial and gender injustice in ways that affirm Black girls' and Black women's humanity" (p. 70). I am the child of a Black woman, an othermother to many children, who, in her spirit, felt so moved to see to it that young people in our community had numerous educational, recreational, and spiritual opportunities for learning. As my mother's daughter, I owe my commitments to critical civic praxis, youth development, and culturally relevant and Afrocentric education directly to my mother, who believed we should acknowledge and cherish who we are as Black people, first, embrace African-centered collectivist traditions out of which our culture was born, and identify the utility of our cultural commitments to, if nothing else, do what is possible to sustain community. Born of a mother who is a pianist, the daughter of a preacher and a teacher, and a woman who served as a community youth director and Minister of Music, my research, teaching, and youth work is undoubtedly influenced by my mother's fighting spirit.

In our book circle discussions that broached cultural memory, ancestral gifts, and mothers' legacies, I found space to interrogate how my mother's many roles deepened my understanding of the complexities of cultural and familial aspects of the research community I have been so privileged to enter. Further, the cultural and spiritual context in which my childhood was situated, and all the associated activities therein ran parallel to and collided with the standard public education I received. On Sundays, we studied a word that my mother and grandmother interpreted as service and sacrifice. Monday through Friday, I studied intensively words that would prepare me to compete in the *real world*. What I have learned from looking back on my doctoral student tenure, however, is that the competitive, openly hostile nature of the academy in and of itself is enough to break what is left of the love and deep spiritual and material commitments we have to ourselves and our students, and to the communities we strive to serve through our work as teachers, researchers, and community-engaged scholars. We do this despite knowing that our hyper(in)visibility (Curtis, 2021) decreases the amount of air around us that we need to survive. Still, I feel compelled to ask how our intellectual undertakings sustain us in places where we are actively being erased?

Some of the cruelest encounters I experienced as a doctoral student reminded me of how all of us who are working in the academy, in many ways, are participating in institutional cultures that perpetuate the marginalization of and dominance over women's, especially Black women's, ways of knowing and being as we wrestle with meeting the excessive demands of teaching and research (Dortch, 2020; Gay, 2004).

Recognizing the depth and breadth of Black women's intellectual and academic pursuits, I caution myself not to lean into an essentialist view of Black women's experiences, social identities, and political standpoints. However, the very essence of striving to obtain "enough" of a certain type of knowledge and academic currency to consider oneself an active scholar with a viable career creates tensions when we try to approach this work from epistemological standpoints rooted in an Africana culture of collective advancement (Collins, 2000; Evans-Winters, 2015, 2019,) or in Black and/or endarkened feminist methodologies that traverse the metaphysical and the spiritual (Dillard, 2000). Reading these frameworks as paradigms for feminist and Afrocentric ways of democratic learning and living (hooks, 2003; Jackson & Howard, 2014), I am reminded of the critical responsibility we have to attempt to restore and sustain our wholeness even if the spaces around us are broken.

Building a Legacy Through Critical Civic Praxis

In our book circle, we encountered Morrison's (2019) essay "The Foreigner's Home." In a discussion on the challenges of globalization, the lack of distinction between the public and private sector (and the private domain of the home), and the implications of a racially and economically stratified society, Morrison makes tangible the sense of "our uneasiness with our own feelings of foreignness, our own rapidly fraying sense of belonging" (p. 8), as she explores the tensions between how we imagine our loyalties to family, culture, country, race, gender, nationality, and so forth. She asks, "How do we decide where we belong?" I recognize that many of the spaces we move in are resistant to the work we, as critical feminist scholars, attempt to do. I often wrestle with the contradictions I feel about my own commitments to understanding the civic identity development and political socialization processes of Black girls who are actively constructing and implementing social action solutions to problems they have identified as being of particular concern to their communities.

My research asks young, Black, civically active girls to reflect on how they see themselves within a historical and contemporary legacy of Black women's politics and social action despite my knowing their lives are situated within a white supremacist, heteropatriarchal societal structure that compels them to social action in their childhood. Knowing young people need safe and culturally affirming spaces just to exist joyfully as children, there were many times throughout my dissertation journey when I experienced conflicting emotions about this work. I spent many hours determining how best to construct opportunities for young people to dialogue, analyze, and critique ideas about democratic practice. This also included ensuring they felt safe and empowered to debate or reject these ideas, particularly when they expressed their displeasure with politics and asserted not feeling welcomed in politicized spaces, such as in schools where political discourse or debate sometimes occurred. Tensions that emerged in the research resulted from my own sense of dislocation as a Black woman who also felt isolated on campus and suffered from similar racial and gendered micro- and macro-aggressions the girls were experiencing in their schools.

Although the research I was conducting was conceptualized using Black feminist and Afrocentric education frameworks, there were times I was grappling with being unable to make sense of my own experiences as teacher, researcher, and big sister in ways that would help me navigate the social and political pressures that continued to press upon my life, upon Black life, and continuously dampened any joy or excitement I should have been experiencing as I neared the end of my doctoral program. Sometimes, I critically questioned if this was the *right* work to do. In what ways did my research offer up a space for sisterly interaction and societal critique in the midst of a new unveiling of systemic oppression, disregard for the loss of Black life, and run towards political ideologies designed to continuously strip away power from our communities?

Daughtering as Identity and Process

Returning to some of the core ideas we dissected in our book circle, particularly surrounding Morrison's (2019) discussion of how Africans and African Americans have to contend with "not being at home in one's homeland" (p. 8) and to Evans-Winter's (2019) illustration of how as daughters "we are taught how to observe the unseen, contemplate the ignored, interpret the forgotten, and analyze the taken for granted, and speak the forbidden" (p. 139), I moved more deeply into the understanding of how research related to the political socialization and civic life of Black girls, and Black youth more broadly, is necessary (Brown, 2007; Woodson & Love, 2019). Drawing on the lessons my mother and grandparents instilled in me and leaning into the lessons I learn from young people's stories, centering the spiritual within critical civic praxis in which the public (society) and private (spiritual) domains intersect at multiple turns, provides a more critical view into how the work I do as a community-engaged scholar. In my work, this is essential to how democratic praxis is conceptualized and to how we can construct our own radical spaces for Black girls and Black women's liberation, healing, and societal transformation (hooks, 1990).

Centering the Spiritual as Ritual and Civic Praxis

In our book circle, I had the privilege of witnessing my sister scholars so bravely sharing their stories, culling memories of their ancestors, their mothers, and their grandmothers, and offering up remedies for coping with troubled times. I thought to myself *what beauty there was residing in their deepest wells*, realizing that during my dissertation journey, I had not always remembered to draw on the women in my life who, despite all they endured, found ways to survive. By the time I was making the final revisions to my dissertation, our scheduled book circle meetings had ended. It was at this stage where, in beginning to write my dedication and acknowledgments, I was able to more clearly articulate how my mother had really influenced and shaped how I felt about the work I was doing. Previously, I had written about how she had influenced my own commitments to working with young people in the first chapter of my dissertation, but those words did not capture the depth of the emotional intelligence and cultural insights she had poured into me and other children in such a way that I had the wherewithal, strength, compassion, empathy, and foresight to enter into community with other youth workers and the young people to whom they dedicated their time and energy. When I look back on how my mother and her parents before her created a home for us in a place where they initially did not have roots by staying with, learning from, and serving others, I am so moved by the tireless energy they had to keep overcoming.

Morrison (2019) writes of home as "memory and companions and/or friends who share the memory" (p. 17). Reading Morrison's words with my sister scholars helped me to reflect on the home my mother created and the home I am making in the place I have now given 10 years—10 years of growth, new experiences, and most importantly, time for critical love and fellowship with community. When I was younger, I used to reflect on the physical environment of my childhood home—its clear skies and fiery sunsets—but I know now it is the memories I look back on now so fondly that call me back to that space much, in the same way, it is the beginning of new memories calling me to the place I now call home. As I reflect back on our book circle gatherings and on the research I conducted at a time in which our lives were continuously marked by state violence and a global health crisis, I recognize that my engagement in any co-constructed civic or political activity with Black girls must center opportunities for young people to feel at home and to cultivate joy in ways that are rooted in the cultural and spiritual ethos of the communities from which we emerge (Dillard, 2000; Evans-Winters, 2015).

Because I had become so entrenched in ensuring I understood what was technically required of me to make it in this line of work, I had suppressed the spiritual foundations I had buried within myself that I needed to sustain myself. In coming to terms with my reality, remembered how my foremothers got over and what, through their survival, I now possessed as ritual and resource. In centering daughtering and Black feminist praxis as identity, method, and process, I see how our Black women's book circle became, for me, a healing place, and a space in which I could invoke the past to construct a way forward, and conceptualize a future not devoid of the spiritual insight and practices I already embodied yet managed to minimize along my professional academic journey.

Black Women's Mental Wealth

Doing this introspective and intellectual work within our book circle illuminated for me how my mother ensured I know who I am, even when I feel there is no definitive pathway home. These acts of (re)membering (Dillard, 2018) tie us to the legacy of Black women whose relentless pursuit of liberation has direct implications for our current political realities—women like Harriet Tubman, Septima Clark, Fannie Lou Hamer, and many other women whose names we don't know, but whose cultural and political legacies we carry. The dialogue we shared about our mothers' lives and the choices they made intersected with our own lived experiences pushed me to think more deeply about how sustaining our cultural and spiritual ethos centers on developing young people's critical and cultural consciousness, protecting their lives, and creating spaces for them to exist as their full selves (Brown, 2007; Ginwright, 2007, 2010; Ginwright & Cammarota, 2007).

Much in the same way, my engagement in the book circle showed me how daughtering (Evans-Winters, 2019) and *Black women's mental wealth* (Evans-Winters, 2020) was a manifestation of a Black feminist ethic of care. In this space, I felt a deeper sense of connection and belonging in ways I had not felt in many years since I left home more than 10 years ago. The conscious choices we made to recall what our mothers and our grandmothers had imparted on us forced me to unbury what had stayed with me despite not knowing how to bring it to the surface. Remembering the lessons my mother taught me is a gift, a foundation on which to restore the spiritual in my critical civic work.

Some of the stories shared in our book circle are sacred, and I never imagined that releasing them would allow me to reclaim my spiritual center. Stepping outside of my academic institution and into this radically creative space clarified for me the point from which I felt dislocated as a Black woman in the academy. I know sharing parts of my journey here on this page further exposes me to additional scrutiny to which Black women are routinely subjected—the paradox of our hyper(in)visibility makes our storytelling both compelling and compromising. But this story is for my sisters who carry a heavy load. Unbury what has carried you. As we journey through complex and often difficult pathways into and through academia, we can still find ourselves and each other, carve out space, and begin anew.

REFERENCES

Brown, R. N. (2007). Remembering Maleesa: Theorizing Black girl politics and the politicizing of socialization. In G. Persons (Ed.), *The expanding boundaries of Black politics* (pp. 121–136). Transaction Publishers.

Collins, P. H. (2000). *Black feminist thought*. Routledge.

Curtis, S. J. (2021). *Black girls' political literacies: The dialectics of civic practice* [Doctoral Dissertation, George Washington University]. ProQuest Dissertations Publishing, 28547685.

Dillard, C. B. (2018). Let steadfastness have its full effect: (Re)membering (re)search and endarkened feminisms from Ananse to Asantewaa. *Qualitative Inquiry, 24*(9), 617–623.

Dillard, C. B. (2000). The substance of things hoped for, the evidence of things not seen: Examining an endarkened feminist epistemology in educational research and leadership. *International Journal of Qualitative Studies in Education, 13*(6), 661–681.

Dillard, C. B., Abdur-Rashid, D. I., & Tyson, C. A. (2000). My soul is a witness: Affirming pedagogies of the spirit. *International Journal of Qualitative Studies in Education, 13*(5), 447–462.

Dortch, D. (2020). Revolutionary Acts: African American doctoral students exercising racial agency at a predominantly white institution of higher education in the United States. *International Journal for Cross-Disciplinary Subjects in Education (IJCDSE)*, *11*(1), 4236–4244.

Evans-Winters, V. E. (2015). Black feminism in qualitative education research: A mosaic for interpreting race, class, and gender in education. In V. E. Evans-Winters & B. L. Love (Eds.), *Black feminism in education: Black women speak back, up, and out* (pp. 129–142). Peter Lang,

Evans-Winters, V. (2019). *Black feminism in qualitative inquiry: A mosaic for writing our daughter's body*. The New Press.

Greene, M. (2000). Imagining futures: The public school and possibility. *Journal of Curriculum Studies*, *32*(2), 267–280.

Ginwright, S. A. (2007). Black youth activism and the role of critical social capital in Black community organizations. *American Behavioral Scientist*, *51*(3), 403–418.

Ginwright, S. A. (2010). *Black youth rising: Activism and radical healing in urban America*. Teachers College Press.

Ginwright, S. A., & Cammarota, J. (2007). Youth activism in the urban community: Learning critical civic praxis within community organizations. *International Journal of Qualitative Studies in Education*, *20*(6), 693–710.

Guy-Sheftall, B. (1995). *Words of fire: An anthology of African-American feminist thought*. The New Press.

hooks, b. (1987). Talking back. *Discourse*, 123–128.

hooks, b. (1991). Theory as liberatory practice. *Yale Journal of Law & Feminism*, *4*(1), 1–12.

hooks, b. (1994). *Teaching to transgress*. Routledge.

hooks, b. (2003). *Teaching community: A pedagogy of hope*. Routledge.

Jackson, T. O., & Howard, T. C. (2014). The continuing legacy of freedom schools as sites of possibility for equity and social justice for black students. *Western Journal of Black Studies*, *38*(3), 155.

Love, B. (2016). Anti-Black state violence, classroom edition: The spirit murdering of Black children. *Journal of Curriculum and Pedagogy*, *13*(1), 22–25.

Morrison, T. (2019). *The source of self-regard: Selected essays, speeches, and meditations*. Alfred A. Knopf.

Muhammad, G., & Haddix, M. (2016). Centering Black girls' literacies: A review of literature on the multiple ways of knowing of Black girls. *English Education*, *48*(4), 299–336.

Pinar, W. F. (2012). *What is curriculum theory?* Routledge.

Twale, D. J., Weidman, J. C., & Bethea, K. (2016). Conceptualizing socialization of graduate students of color: Revisiting the Weidman-Twale-Stein framework. *Western Journal of Black Studies*, *40*(2), 80–94.

Walker, A. (1983). *In search of our mothers' gardens*. Harcourt.

Woodson, A. N., & Love, B. L. (2019). Outstanding: Centering Black kids' enoughness in civic education research. *Multicultural Perspectives*, *21*(2), 91–96.

CHAPTER 7

AM I MY SISTAH'S KEEPER? OR, A BROKEN WORKHORSE?

Escape Route: Paying the Price to Avoid Whiteness

La'Keisha Gray-Sewell

Am I My Sistah's Keeper? Or a Broken Workhorse? examines the experiences that Black women face when we escape white supremacy and take refuge in Black community workspaces. As Black women, many of our adverse childhood experiences (ACEs) are experienced within institutions that uphold white supremacy. Under the instruction of teachers, the crippling admonishment of judges, or the unyielding barriers of corporate executives, our humanity is devalued. We act as shields and advocates for our constituents. The emotional wear and tear are detrimental to our overall wellness. We resist by reserving our intellectual, emotional, and artistic gifts for our community. Often, our service is not compensated with living wages that ensure our livelihood. This chapter draws upon reflections on Black sanctuary and how sisterhood was used to cope with an economic crisis amid mass death and racial battle fatigue during a pandemic.

Black Women Mothering & Daughtering During a Dual Pandemic: Writing Our Backs, pp. 75–84
Copyright © 2024 by Information Age Publishing
www.infoagepub.com

THIS THING CALLED LIFE

April 4, 2020

To know me is to understand, I'm real …
Passionate. Brave. Clumsy. Awkward. Insecure. Intelligent. Doubtful. Walking by Faith. A Believer. Genuine. A perfectly flawed human contradiction.
I am Spirit. The Most High living and breathing.

What you see is what you get, plus layers to it.
No pretense. Never pretending it.

I've been honest enough
To put a bow on another's gifts
Wrap it with the bow and place back in the rightful hands
Given the proper credit

I've practiced mercy and grace.
Could've told the truth
About you and the situation
But never said it.

Had beef but never cooked it.
Yeah, I like it raw, so I give it to the universe
Let Karma deal with it.

I've learned my share of lessons.
Life is the hand we've been dealt with.
Live it to the fullest. Make peace with your past and the conditions you
started with.
No regretting it.

Write the wrongs.
Honor the Principles
All 12 have meaning.
Forgive and request forgiveness.
Any harm or hurt, heal it.

This time, these moments are all that is promised.
Won't let death steal it;
Not by tongue.
Not by deed.
Not by mind.
Mind over matter…
Any Dis-Ease, plague or pandemic
That's how you kill it.

But life … all you can do is live it.

In January 2020, news of a pandemic had begun. By March, we were in total lockdown and closed in our homes. We were forced to make space for ourselves within our otherwise busy, overwhelmed lives. Then, with nowhere to look away, we witnessed a series of Black lynchings on our screens. My mind retreated to 1984.

Circa 1984

My fourth-grade year of elementary school was filled with days of wonder and discovery. That classroom was where my love for animals deepened. It was where my classmates and I nurtured a baby bird that a fellow student had rescued. The class named it Robert, and we got it well enough until it grew feathers and could fly away. Our teacher, Mrs. Nolan, was a part-time veterinarian and nature lover. She escorted us on walking trips to study the fall leaves and their trees of origin. In the classroom, she hosted tea parties where we tested our five senses using sassafras teas, citrus, and other items that brought our imagination alive. She thrilled us with her academic lessons. Still, inside this same classroom and under the governance of this same teacher, each day, I had to learn a different kind of lesson: a lesson of survival. I had to learn to tuck in pieces of myself because whenever I expressed disappointment, frustration, or displeasure, I was berated and reprimanded. Mrs. Nolan defined my display of emotion as sulking. She frequently demanded conferences with my mother to discuss my "attitude."

It was almost as bad as the year before. That year, I made the daily march into a Willis Wagon (Blakemore, 2024) for third-grade instruction. Initially, in the early 1960s, to enable segregation of public schools, aluminum mobile units—also known as trailers—were ordered by Superintendent Benjamin Willis. Speaking about systemic racism, community organizer Bob Lucas surmised the public opinion in stating, "When a Black school that was close to a white school became overcrowded, rather than permitting the Black kids to cross a block and go to the white schools, the Willis Wagons were put up on the campuses of the Black schools to contain them."

Twenty years later, I found my peers, and I were assigned to those same Willis Wagon classrooms. Something about being isolated from the main school building didn't feel right to me. While my 8-year-old brain could not articulate my discontent, what was clear was how my teacher treated me and my primarily remains Hispanic classmates. The trauma from one incident, in particular, remain with me today. I had been raising my hand for permission to go to the restroom. My teacher ignored me for some time and then questioned my honesty. When she finally relented to let me go, I could no longer hold my bladder. It released, and urine seeped through my white pants. Humiliated, I sat at my desk for the remainder of the day and then walked the mile home with my clothes wet with urine.

Then, in high school, my family had temporarily moved to a Chicago south suburb. The relocation meant I had to attend the district high school, which was predominantly white with even fewer Black faculty. Dauntingly, the administration presented hurdle after hurdle before admitting me. They demanded my mother produce proof of address. Then, they requested divorce papers to prove custody. As a student, my White music teacher seemed to delight in ostracizing and humiliating me almost daily. These instances greatly contrast the sense of belonging and community I felt in the Black schools I attended, like Anthony Overton Elementary School and Walter H. Dyett Middle School in the historic Bronzeville community on Chicago's South Side.

Throughout the years, over and over again, from elementary school through high school, college, and the workforce, scenario after scenario confirmed a belief for me: White spaces are dangerous for girls like me. Granted, it may have been subconscious, but the consequence of this belief led me to seek harbor in workspaces and services that offered familiar cultural idiosyncrasies—spaces where language, expression, and manners were held together by a common thread. Unbeknownst to me, that common thread would be a spiritual connection weaved in Black womanist literature and theory. As Akasha Gloria Hull (2001) prophetically offered:

> I further believe that African American women, specifically, have a crucial role to play in this transmission of spiritual consciousness, clearly seen first in the rise of supernatural and esoteric content in their literature during the 1980s. This mission, if you will, is still apparent in the awareness with which progressive African American women are living their lives. (p. 186)

It began simply enough. I found myself searching for soul retreats away from white instruction, and I guess you could include the viciousness of teenage angst and cattiness. The school library was an obvious place to go. There, I got lost in Maya Angelou's (1997) *I Know Why the Caged Bird Sings*. I related deeply to girl Maya's state of dissonance in response to the oppressive white world around her. Naturally, I progressed along her trajectory into womanhood, thus devouring her entire autobiographical series. During my school years and beyond, Maya's life philosophy and choices became a useful blueprint to help me navigate my girlhood into Black womanhood, taking on many roles as social justice activist, mentor, mother, wife, community servant, friend, and daughter. Maya's stories paved the path toward Alice Walker's words. And Zora Neale Hurston. And Paule Marshall. And Toni Morrison. And Terri McMillan. And Pearl Cleage. And *Essence Magazine*. The characters and storylines illuminated the magic of the Black women's experiences. Their words saved my life and gave me a space to always run to.

This journey ushered me into a life assignment to create a culturally relevant space where Black girls are liberated and free. Eventually, in 2012, I founded Girls Like Me Project Inc. (G.L.M.P.I.), a community-based not-for-profit that serves Black girls. Our mission is to help African American girls ages 11–17 critically examine social, cultural, and political ideologies in media so that they will be able to overcome stigmas and negative stereotypes. We equip them with the tools and strategies to become influential, independent digital storytellers who transform their communities and foster global sisterhood.

Notwithstanding the unapologetic intention of our mission, insulating Black girls in a safe space that edifies, affirms, and connects them to their identity as Blackness is intentional. Inherently, it is yet another strategy for safety. So much so that it would not be hyperbole to declare it a cultural preserving and ultimately lifesaving strategy.

As twisted fate would have it, the necessity of this approach became explicitly clear during the transcendent unfolding of 2020. Our girls were hit with devastating combination punches of a viral pandemic and related deaths, racial battles, social isolation, and economic strangulation. Without hesitation, I sounded the alarm for all girl-serving organizations in Chicago, specifically the Chicago Coalition on Urban Girls members, to build out COVID-19 response programming. Our efforts were to supplement programming and fill gaps created by closed schools and stressed families.

I understood the power of G.L.M.P.I.'s unique programming when I started the organization. Nonetheless, I could have never foreseen how critical our social programs would be in a society that shows deference to girls' programming that emphasizes traditional mentoring services like academic enforcement or etiquette. Our core pedagogy of media literacy, storytelling, sisterhood, herstory (contributions of women's history), and Sankofa transitioned seamlessly into an online curriculum that addressed the very real and present issues families were experiencing. Thus, we built a curriculum that prioritized community-centered solutions and provided Black girls with the social-emotional tools to navigate their new bizarre world of pronounced racial inequity and thick death. The need we were resolving had been predicted by Michelle Russell (1977) over four decades ago in stating:

> Robbed of all other continuities, prohibited free expression, and denied a written history for centuries by white America, Black people have been driven to rely on oral recitation for our sense of the past. Today, however, the tradition is under severe attack. Urban migration, apartment living, mass-media dependency, and the break-up of generational within units the family have corroded our ability to renew our community through oral

forms. History becomes what's in the books. Authority depends on the academic credentials on the academic credentials that follow after one's name
or the dollar amount of one's paycheck: the distance one has traveled....
Significant categories of time are defined by television's thirty-second spots
or thirty-minute features. (p. 2)

For G.L.M.P.I., this shows up in our Digitally Innovative Voices of Advocacy Sisters in the City (D.I.V.A.S. in the City) program. The primary focus
of D.I.V.A.S. is training girls in media literacy and digital storytelling. We
expose girls to media that feature the intersectionality of Black women
represented as filmmakers, producers, actors, and key players in the media
landscape. Moreover, the goal is to ensure girls understand the power of
owning their narratives and the impact of seeing reflections of their lived
experiences validated on screen. In as much, we reveal media has a role as
an advocacy tool and social shifter.

Consequently, girls are guided in critical analysis of media messages and
images. During the Summer of COVID-19, we held film screenings of *Black
is King* (2020) and a watch party for Girl Trek's *Daughters Of* (n.d.), a monu-
mental conversation with Angela Davis and Nikki Giovanni. Another facet
of our COVID-19 programming was a shift to immune-fortifying wellness
lessons. Early on, we started livestream workshops, including topics such
as yoga, fitness, growing microgreens, aromatherapy, and dance. These
activities were efforts to prevent the spread of COVID-19 throughout our
families, especially because many of our girls lived with multiple generations of their families and were close to essential workers.

With this in mind, we also expanded our programming to include
socially-distanced versions of our Sankofa nights throughout the Summer.
The intention of these block-club-style pop-ups was to infuse intergenerational traditions to promote peace and community healing.

Because of COVID-19, we added a mutual aid component. Each event
featured the distribution of personal protective equipment and fresh food
offerings, mindfulness programming (e.g., yoga, gardening & martial arts),
spoken word, dance presentations, African drumming, drum line, film
screenings, hand games, double dutch, a live D.J., and virtual reality games.

What I knew for sure was how vital it was for me to remain on an ele-
vated conscious level in order to serve from a higher place than what was
happening within the public psyche. My practice had a deep knowledge
among and of Black women and girls. Little did I know my decision long
ago to find refuge in the confines of Black space would come with a high
toll to pay.

No doubt, the brutal force of dual pandemics, a global health pandemic, and racial injustices in 2020 punctuated this reality for many of us
doing the heavy lifting and space-keeping. I finally sought professional

support from a Black woman therapist. The tools to journal, self-reflective questions, and calming exercises helped me recall the trauma from my childhood classrooms. Participating in video calls with this Black woman, I recognized a sister I could confide in and who understood me on a soul level. She helped me explore how so many of us have normalized struggle and suffering as living. Finally, therapy and digging deeper into my first love of writing completed my soul retreats. Summarily, sharing my work with my community in an otherwise isolated time period provided an outlet for anxiety and low-grade depression. Through these practices and sanctuary with my Black sister comrades in the literature circle restored my peace and created space to thrive. In doing so, I brought my girls and their families along to higher ground. Conclusively, writing the poems below helped sustain me during my most painful times during 2020.

IN CHICAGO THEY SING THE BLUES

July 10, 2020

Not talking Koko Taylor or even Stax Records

I'm talking about the nightly news

Where they love to tell you

How many got shot. And identify the deadliest blocks.

Without ever bothering to walk through

And see the life being lived cause we don't claim death.

What they won't tell you Is how many brilliant youth

Got accepted to HBCU's

Competed in robotics teams or embarked on their dreams

To be a STEM rockstar

Or the block clubs full of old school love

Mentors providing structure while organizers form like Voltron to redirect, fill in the gaps To address and correct every wrong

Including poverty and systemic racism, the culprit that got us here.

No no no they'd rather bamboozle and hook us with the blues

They cover up 16 shots leaving baby dead by bad boys in Blue Won't show you beauty in the hood

Murals on walls left vacant from corporate divestment.

They won't show you Ghetto Gardens in bloom

Their melody never includes

Neighbors bringing out the African drum and djembes so the rhythm reminds us where we come from

They won't play the song

Of how many babies are born, string together a harmony of life

Despite what it looks like

Because according to the news,

We are all devastated

No hope Wallowing in despair

None of us with Black skin really cares

There aren't people on the south and west side

Just homicide

But we are here!

Listen to our melody of self-love and determination

We are here

Listen to our spirituals resilience

We spread the truth like Gospel

Supporting small business and entrepreneurs

Practicing those good old village values

Because we are much more than the blues

FROM THE CRADLE TO THE GRAVE

July 31, 2020

Since conception there has been a perception
That my life was of no matter ... nor consequence.
Policies and agenda in place
With the explicit goal to erase
My humanity.

Sexual liberation and planned parenthood
Except for the sisters in the hood ...
The would be mamas.
Margaret Sanger presumed a Black woman's womb was unfit.

So equipped with policy and science she became the architect of eugenics.

Yet somehow we make it through
Mama's egg and Daddy's sperm
Conception resumed

Now what about the quality of prenatal care
Mama and baby need fresh, healthy food
But they live in a food desert.
Guess that means baby is born premature.

Or underweight.

Just trying to make a way
Not even $15 in minimum wage
Can't raise a family with no cents
In an environment full of structural violence
Lead in drinking water
Asbestos and construction dust in air
Asthmatic lungs constricted
Housing options restricted
By race and red lines

Somebody throw a lifeline
I would pull up the straps
But I lost the boots for mine
Somewhere across the waters of the Transatlantic Slave Trade
Looking at the inequity, one percent got it made
I just want to live life to become a ripe old age
Yet in Englewood life expectancy is barely 60
Up north they get nine decades
And lots of urban planning and development green space.

Imagine that.
No really ... imagine that.
Close your eyes and visualize
Feel what it must be like to know from the moment you were thought of
Whether in lust or love
An entire system was designed for you to fail
Early death or in jail
Opportunity rigged

School doors closed Poverty
socially engineered History
deceptively hidden
Indigenous or Black skin
Proof of your ancestor's powers

Evident every time you win

Because they can't stop you.
It's in your DNA
No matter the evil plans.

No matter the narrative
Overcome the trauma.
Overcome the stereotypes and stigma
Overcome adversity through resilience
You will win
From the cradle to the grave.
You matter.

REFERENCES

Angelou, M. (1997). *I know why the caged bird sings*. Bantam Books.

Beyoncé, Adjei, E., Bazawule, B., Debusschere, P., Nkiru, J., Ake, I., Rimmasch, D., & Nava, J. (Directors). (2020). *Black is king* [Film]. Walt Disney Pictures Parkwood Entertainment.

Blakemore, E. (2024). *Why MLK encouraged 225,000 kids to cut class in 1963*. History. https://www.history.com/news/chicago-public-school-boycott-1963-freedom-movement-mlk

Girl Trek. (n.d.). *We are the #Daughters Of our ancestors' wildest dreams*. https://www.girltrek.org/act/daughters-of/

Gray-Sewell, L. (2020, April). *This thing called life*.

Gray-Sewell, L. (2020, July). *From the cradle to the grave*.

Gray-Sewell, L. (2020, July). *In Chicago they sing the blues*.

Hull, A. G. (2001). *Soul talk*. Simon & Schuster.

Russell, M. (1977). Black eyed blues collection: Teaching Black women. *Women Studies Quarterly, 4*(4).

AFTERWORD

MORE THAN ENOUGH

Joy Lawson Davis

Fierce but compassionate, dynamic but focused, looking back while always looking ahead, the authors of this unique text are setting the record straight. We are more than enough to excel in any environment, at any time, to change outcomes for the least of society—including the disenfranchised Black community and others held in the same disregard. During one of our nation's most vulnerable times, Black women scholars have shown up again and again—to demonstrate their "why." Why, we have always been known to rise to the occasion and rise and rise and rise again. This text describes how the voices of exemplary scholars who rose above the dual pandemics we all experienced. These chapters are like intimate testimonials often shared out loud, resulting in our understanding that we are blessed to be a blessing to others.

The intersectional identities of scholars, mothers, daughters, and sisters work to heal others while often in stages of recovering the lived experience of Black women scholars' complex, but not undoable. These scholars have descended from others who have sacrificed heart, soul, mind, and body for generations to create and nurture our communities through unseen and seen dangers. In communities across the nation, Black females have held the simultaneous roles of sister, daughter, matriarch, mother, Queen, and the infamous "auntie," providing support with a depth of understanding and protection that none other across cultures and genders could understand.

While reading, I felt the reality of these Black women scholars as descendants of the Warrior Women of West Africa. So many of us are. We take our ancestry seriously and are committed to carrying the legacy of strength, ungendered ingenuity, and deep and abiding love onward to help our people gain their rightful place in history. I was so moved and inspired while reading each of these chapters. The pain experienced by some was as palpable as the victory and success felt by others. The empathy that arose in my heart while reading the authors' testimonials wanted me to reach out and do what I could to help. Isn't that what we always do?

The recent dual pandemics brought out the best in many of us. These stories of survival during the ongoing health and economic pandemics are so familiar. As a lifelong scholar of equity and advocacy, I applaud these courageous authors for writing their experiences so that others can be affirmed on their own journeys. Their essays are like the stories of so many that have been unheard. What a priceless gift to have.

This text takes its readers down the winding road of what it means to be a Black woman in society today. It describes the stories of Black women who felt increasing pressure not only to survive but to thrive during two of our nation's most historically devastating pandemics. During these dual pandemics, the Black community was disproportionately victimized. These scholars responded by digging deep and creating programs that were instructive and supportive to themselves and the wider community.

In each essay, the authors express what it feels like to be a Black woman as the universal/eternal protector and real-life superhero. Those to whom the world looks to save, salvage, create, reform, feed, and protect, generation to generation. What these authors found within their group is the strength of the sisterhood support that is often not available in predominantly white environments. Their sisterhood empowered them to reach deep within and share their sometimes painful experiences of mothering and daughtering "on their backs".

These essays also provide visual images of the challenges of being Black females throughout the generations. Within the chapters, I envisioned the enslaved maid seated and feeding not only her offspring, but those of the slave masters as well. Because whatever we do for ourselves always seems to benefit the "others" as well. As a reader, you also experienced rituals from the African diaspora that give our community what seems like secret supernatural strength and wisdom to face challenges yet unknown to others.

Throughout this book, the scholars define the deep sense of responsibility we feel to lift and carry our community to the top of the mountain. Like the mythical Sisyphus, the boulder we push rolls back each time we are delayed or stumble on the climb. The pandemics created multiple and simultaneous delays and stumbling blocks. This volume demonstrates that, despite the interruptions, we have the capacity to push the boulder until it reaches the top. These scholars pushed the boulder and changed the image to one we do not see often enough—Black mothers and daughters reaching the pinnacle of one of the many mountains they must climb.

The authors of these chapters are the offspring of brave, courageous women who dreamt daily of a life of freedom, streets to walk on in peace, institutions to be educated, spaces to have their voices be heard, their ideas be manifested, their children nurtured as the best, and their visions of the future come to pass. When confronted with the dangers of the dual pandemics, these authors drew from the deep wells of this ancestry to "keep on keeping on."

These are the ancestors who walked invisible ivy halls, spoke in unheard lecture halls, and existed in spaces their ancestors built. These essays are a revelation for some and a cleansing for others. Each chapter speaks for itself. Subsequently, the chapters are tied together with common themes, creating a unified text for coursework use. This text would be an excellent choice for a primary or supplemental textbook for university courses that address Black family engagement, cultural diversity, access, culturally responsive pedagogy, Black feminism, and social justice. This range of topics makes this a powerful book for analyzing ethnographic research.

What a precious gift these erudite scholars have given us. Black women have once again demonstrated that our "why" is more than enough to set the pace for others to learn from, live by, and emulate.

ABOUT THE AUTHORS

Venus E. Evans-Winters, LCSW, PhD, Venus E. Evans-Winters, PhD, is the Black Girls Initiatives Research Coordinator at the African American Policy Forum. She is also a Visiting Professor of Education at The Ohio State University. Her areas of research are educational policy analysis, Black girls' and women's onto-epistemologies, and critical race feminist methodologies. She is the author of *Black Feminism in Qualitative Inquiry: A Mosaic for Writing Our Daughter's Body* and *Teaching Black Girls: Resilience in Urban Schools* and co-author of *Introduction to Intersectional Qualitative Research*. She is co-editor of the books, *Black Feminism in Education: Black Women Speak Up, Back, & Out* and *Celebrating Twenty Years of Black Girlhood: The Lauryn Hill Reader.* Dr. Evans-Winters is also a clinical psychotherapist in private practice and the founder of Planet Venus Institute.

Amber Jean Marie Pabon, PhD, is an Associate Professor of Urban Education at Kutztown University of Pennsylvania. A former secondary English teacher with degrees in sociocultural anthropology and English education, Dr. Pabon earned her doctorate at City University, New York. She leads several campus cabinets, including as the chairs of Diversity and Equity in the College of Education and General Education Assessment. In addition, she is the founder/director of Emerging Educators of Color—a program to recruit and retain BIPOC educators to teach in urban schools. In fall 2022, Dr. Pabon began directorship of the Frederick Douglass Institute at Kutztown University. Dr. Pabon's scholarship focuses on the life histories and schooling experiences of Black teachers and Black youth. It has been published in *Race, Ethnicity, and Education, Equity, Excellence and Education,*

Urban Education, *Education Studies*, and *Urban Review*. She has presented her research at conferences, including Educational Studies, the National Council of Teachers of English, the American Educational Research Association, the International Conference on Urban Education, and the World Education Research Association.

Theresa Y. Robinson, PhD, is an Associate Professor and Director of Secondary & PK–12 at Elmhurst University. She is also the Founder and Executive Director of The George Washington Carver: Center for the Advancement of Science. Dr. Robinson earned a B.S. in Biological Sciences and Secondary Education and Ph.D. in Curriculum and Instruction with an emphasis in science and environmental education. She taught grades 9–12 science in Chicago Public Schools. She has dedicated her career to dismantling inequity in STEM education, preparing teachers to use culturally relevant and sustaining pedagogies, and providing STEM professional development to PK–12 teachers. She is a founding member of the Black Education Advocacy Coalition, an active member of the National Science Teachers Association, National Association for Research in Science Teaching, American Educational Research Association, and the American Association of Colleges for Teacher Education.

Janice Baines is a Clinical Instructor at the University of South Carolina. Janice served as an elementary education teacher for 16 years, specializing in Culturally Relevant Teaching. Her research focuses on African-centered curriculum, Black girls' literacy, and social media education as a Black feminist intervention.

Dyanis Conrad, PhD, is an assistant professor of Equity & Diversity in Education and the Program Coordinator for Education Studies at Randolph-Macon College in Virginia. Her research centers on social and educational inequalities, racial and intercultural literacies, critical social justice, and the deconstruction and disruption of colonial legacies. As a qualitative researcher and consultant, she seeks to explore the effects of racialized and colonized practices on the sociocultural and educational experiences of marginalized populations, to center the perspectives and experiences of historically marginalized communities, and to promote educational policies and practices geared toward improving equity and access for all students.

Angela Clack, PsyD, Dr. Angela Roman Clack is a licensed psychotherapist, international speaker, author, and owner of Clack Associates, LLC, a group private practice in New Jersey. With her extensive training and teaching abilities, Dr. Clack has made a massive impact in her community by reducing the stigma of people of color who seek mental health treatment. Dr. Clack is passionate about mental health and wellness, including women's interests with a passion for treating and assessing anxiety and mood disorders with Black women. She is a mental health subject matter expert in diagnosing, assessing, and treating relational trauma. She is the author of *Women of Color Talk: Psychological Narratives on Trauma and Depression* (2018).

Sabrina J. Curtis, PhD, is Assistant Professor in the Youth and Social Innovation Program in the School of Education and Human Development at the University of Virginia. Her teaching, research, and community-facing work centers on youth civic engagement and sociopolitical development, gender equity in education, Black feminist pedagogies, and the politics of Black girlhood. Sabrina provides consulting on research and curriculum development for out of school time programs and initiatives focused on youth advocacy and life skills for girls of color. She is also the co-founder of The Pyramid Project, a nonprofit leadership development organization serving youth in rural communities.

La'Keisha Gray-Sewell is an author, strategic communications consultant by trade, and girls' advocate by life assignment. La'Keisha founded Girls Like Me Project Inc. to train girls in media literacy and empower them to navigate beyond negative media stereotypes to become global legacy builders. Under her leadership, GLMPI has served more than 700 girls through its transformative programs and events. La'Keisha earned her Bachelor of Science degree in Mass Communications/Radio and Television from Southern Illinois University in Carbondale. She is currently a candidate for the Master of Social Work at the University of Illinois-Chicago Jane Addams College of Social Work.

www.ingramcontent.com/pod-product-compliance
Lightning Source LLC
Chambersburg PA
CBHW050539270326
41926CB00015B/3295